Master Your Fears

Master Your Fears

*How to Triumph over Your Worries
and Get on with Your Life*

LINDA SAPADIN, PH.D.

WILEY

John Wiley & Sons, Inc.

Published by John Wiley & Sons, Inc., Hoboken, New Jersey
Published simultaneously in Canada

For general information about our other products and services, please contact our Customer Care Department within the United States at (800) 762-2974, outside the United States at (317) 572-3993 or fax (317) 572-4002.

Wiley also publishes its books in a variety of electronic formats. Some content that appears in print may not be available in electronic books. For more information about Wiley products, visit our web site at www.wiley.com.

Library of Congress Cataloging-in-Publication Data:

Sapadin, Linda.
  Master your fears : how to triumph over your worries and get on with your life / Linda Sapadin.
    p. cm.
Includes bibliographical references and index.
  ISBN 0-471-27272-8 (cloth)
1. Fear. 2. Self-actualization (Psychology) I. Title.
  BF575.F2S26 2004
  152.4'6—dc22   2003017782

Printed in the United States of America

10 9 8 7 6 5 4 3 2 1

To my husband Ron
and my sons Brian, Glenn, and Daniel,
for their love, support, and enthusiasm

Contents

Acknowledgments xi

Introduction: A Personal Journey 1

PART ONE

Understanding Your Fears

1 Fear as a Way of Life 7

2 The Five Fear Styles 15

3 How a Fearful Lifestyle Develops 29

4 Understanding the Change Process 43

PART TWO

A Program for Change

5 Steps for Managing Your Mind 53

6 Steps for Altering Your Attitudes 77

7 Steps for Enhancing Your Language 95

8 Steps for Transforming Your Speech Patterns 115

9 Steps for Tuning In to Your Body 135

10   Steps for Being Footloose and Fear-Free   155

11   Steps for Acting Your Way Out of Fear   171

12   Steps for Doing One Gutsy Thing   191

PART THREE

Life after Fear

13   Fear Less, Live More: True Stories
      of Metamorphosis   213

14   Other Approaches to Help You
      Master Your Fears   223

Resources   231

Further Reading   235

Index   237

Acknowledgments

In my finer moments, I think of writing a book as a fun project. And for the most part, it is. However, it is also a long and frustrating project during which it is essential to be nurtured and inspired by encouraging people who gently reassure you and prod you beyond your doubts. I have been blessed to have many such people in my life, and it is my pleasure to acknowledge their contributions.

I am especially grateful to Ed Myers, who influenced this book in many ways. Ed, thanks for your excellent insights and advice, your writing and editorial skills, and your encouragement and reassurance. This book is a better book because of all you've done.

I am most appreciative to my agent, Faith Hamlin, for nurturing me throughout the entire writing process. It's a long road from "I've got an idea" to the joyous days of "My book is in print!" Faith, I cherish your continued support and confidence in me.

I am very thankful to my editor, Tom Miller, for his interest in the topic and for his counsel and wisdom. Tom, each recommendation you made has improved and strengthened this book.

Thanks also to Lisa Burstiner, my production editor, and to Amy Handy, my copy editor, for helping to bring this book to print.

Career goals are advanced not only by the professional people in your life, but also by your personal relationships—those significant others who inspire the best in you.

My husband, Ron Goodrich, has always been an ardent supporter of all of my ventures. His influence in this book has been invaluable, contributing ideas, insights, editing, and inspiration. When I am frustrated (and the writing process is a frustrating one) or perplexed about how to handle a matter (which happens more frequently than I'd like to admit), Ron is there for me with an innovative solution and unending patience. Ron, your wisdom, good judgment, and unconditional love means so much to me.

I'd also like to express appreciation to Ron and to my friend Sheila Peck who brainstormed with me on the title and subtitle of this book. It's a joy for me to be able to bounce ideas around with such creative minds.

I don't know if it's possible to be a parent and not have many moments of fear. But I do know, that if you don't inoculate your children with your own fears, they can be your best teachers. My three sons Brian, Glenn, and Daniel, have, each in his own way, taught me much about mastering my fears.

Brian, your enthusiasm for life, your love of music, and your willingness to chart your own course have been an amazing source of inspiration for me.

Glenn, your joy of travel, your enjoyment of the unusual, and your gregarious nature have provided me with extraordinary experiences that I would have been too timid to have on my own.

Danny, your confidence in yourself, your spiritual nature, and your commitment to action have helped me to become a more self-confident person.

Thanks my precious sons, for bringing me so much joy.

To my sister, Ruth Grant—the first kid in our family to have the courage to strike out on her own—thanks for making it easier for me in childhood; thanks for making it easier for me today.

To my brother, Robert Fink—who as a kid, could not help but defy and disobey—thanks for showing me another way to live. Good girls are usually scared girls.

Special thanks to my patients, friends, and family who had the trust in me and the courage in themselves to share their narratives, insights, and viewpoints. Respecting your confidentiality, I have altered identifying information or created composite characters for the stories in this book.

Finally, my appreciation to you, the reader, for your interest in my book. This book is a reflection of a lifetime of questioning, learning, and growing. If you would like to contribute to this body of knowledge, please write to me at DrSapadin@aol.com or visit my Web site at www.DrSapadin.com or www.psychwisdom.com.

Introduction
A Personal Journey

THERE MAY BE SOME KIDS who come into this world with courage, confidence, and guts, but I wasn't one of them. I come from fear. I was born sensitive and shy, and lots of things scared me. I worried about serious things, such as what it's like to be dead and how awful it must be to fight in a war. I worried about what other people thought of me, and I still remember coming home crying because my second-grade teacher, Miss Orr, had accused me of lying. Me! The girl who wanted to please, to do good, to be liked. The kid who would flee to her room and hide under the covers when the world felt too big and threatening. Little did Miss Orr realize that even if I wanted to, I was too scared to lie.

In contrast, today I'm a confident, competent, and courageous adult. I've had experiences that amaze me. Some things are truly unusual, like tracking mountain gorillas in Uganda or appearing on national TV. Others are just brave for me—speaking my mind without worrying about what other people think, disagreeing with an authority figure, or skiing a slope that's a bit beyond me.

Most of the time my fears don't control my actions—if they did, I wouldn't do half the things I've done—nor do they take up a whole lot of space in my brain. I've got better things to think about now. I wouldn't be honest, however, if I told you that all of my fears are a thing of the past. They aren't. Indeed, sometimes I seek out a project that will take me into unexplored territory, which reactivates my old fears. In those moments, I feel both excited and scared to death.

Writing this book is one of those thrilling, apprehensive projects. At this very moment, I'm frightened and frustrated. I wonder why I torture myself with such a big project. I ask myself, "What if I'm in over my head? What if I just can't do it? What if I do it and it's not good enough?" But after this bout with doubt—which rarely lasts more than a few hours—I settle down to work and miraculously the words start flowing. Sometimes it's easy, sometimes it's difficult, but somehow I always seem to regain my confidence and renew my efforts.

Most of us believe that if only we were strong enough to overcome our self-doubt, master our uncertainties, and conquer our fears, we'd be okay. Yet, in our heart we know that our behavior and our emotions are not only dependent on our will but also on the pull and force of the situation we're in. I know that although my life is no longer dominated by fear, fear will visit me from time to time. Sometimes it's a lifesaver. Sometimes it's a welcome friend. Sometimes it's just a pain in the neck. But one thing fear is *not* is a demon that stops me from living life.

I've learned much about mastering fear, and I want to share my knowledge with you. I know how fear can hold you back from being who you could be. I know how fear can grow in darkness and in isolation, even when you have a well-composed exterior. I know how fear can eat away at what you hold dear and destroy it. But I also know that the flip side of fear is excitement, even thrill. I know that there can be joy in facing fear and mastering it rather than being possessed by it.

A while ago, I had lunch with two friends, and we talked about their fear of flying, which had intensified following the terror alerts after September 11. Before long, the topic had moved on to summer vacations. Joanie chatted about the exciting trip to the Grand Canyon that she and her husband had planned.

"It sounds great," said Kim, "but I know how much you're afraid to fly. How are you going to do it?"

"I'm not sure," Joanie replied. "The flight will probably be hell for me. But I've decided not to let it stop me."

"I wish I had your attitude."

"Maybe one day you will. Don't give up on yourself."

"I hope you're right," Kim said with a doubtful sigh.

As I left the restaurant, I thought to myself that the significant difference between people isn't whether they're afraid or not afraid. It's whether they can live fully *despite* the fear they feel. It's whether they're more excited about the adventure than intimidated by the fear.

It's strange that we live in an age in which we're healthier, safer, richer, and living far longer than previous generations ever dreamed of—yet none of that makes us feel safer or less vulnerable. Indeed, it's often true that the more we know, the longer we live, the wealthier we are, the more frightened we feel. Remember the days before seat belts, air bags, and bicycle helmets? Remember the days before we thought every lump and bump could be cancer? Remember the days when wars and atrocities didn't show up daily in your living room? Remember the days when you weren't worried about the stock market—because you had no money to invest? In those days we were actually more vulnerable, yet we were less aware of our vulnerability. We enjoyed life more because we knew less. Now, I'm not suggesting that ignorance is bliss. And I don't believe that we could possibly go back to knowing less. But I *am* suggesting that we need to learn new ways to live an aware life with more courage and less fear.

I have a lot to offer you in this book. I know a great deal about how fear develops, how it is displayed, and, most important, how to change the pattern of fearfulness.

This book has three sections. Part I, "Understanding Your Fears," describes how a fearful lifestyle restricts activities, constricts thinking, pinches choices, and squeezes all the juiciness out of life. I introduce you to five different styles of fear and show how each of those styles affects your mind, voice, body, and actions. Taking the self-assessment quizzes will help you determine your own major fear style.

Part II, "A Program for Change," takes the mystery out of the transformation by providing a skills-based program—learning new ways to think, speak, use your body, and act. In that section, I'll lead you through the skills you'll need to learn how to master your fear and triumph over your worries.

Here's a quick overview of the kinds of skills you'll learn:

Thinking your way out of fear. These skills will help you develop an ability to rethink and reframe how you think about a fearful situation. You'll also learn how to shift from obsessive rumination to solution-oriented thinking. Learning how to assess risk versus reward will be another great asset in helping you make decisions in scary situations.

Speaking your way out of fear. Like worried thinking, worried speech can have a powerful, burdensome effect on your psyche. Habitually speaking to others (and to yourself) with gloomy, fearful, heavy-hearted words creates mental and physical anguish that can be as heavy to bear as bad events you actually live through. By changing the manner in which you speak, you can change the manner in which you live.

Freeing your body from fear. Fear is felt *in the body* in many ways— from a general feeling of tension and tightness to headaches, shoulder pains, and fatigue. Unconscious memories of events and ominous warnings are stored in the body. Indeed, even when the mind doesn't remember, the body does. By using body movement exercises, deep breathing techniques, and music, you can lighten the fear you feel in your body and be more open to what life has to offer.

Acting your way out of fear. Many people believe that courage means feeling no fear. In fact, courageous people do feel fear; however, they have developed an ability to take action *despite* their fear. This section teaches you how to do what must be done *even when it's tough or terrifying.* By learning to take risks in which you may indeed fail, and by surviving the failure anyway, you can work your way out of habitual fearfulness.

Finally, Part III, "Life after Fear" is a motivational and inspirational section. I present real life vignettes of people who have triumphed over their fears. In their own words, they speak about *what made the difference for them.* They will share with you how they learned to live in the world without fear as their driving force, and how, when they did, their lives became much sweeter. This part also explains when you should consider seeking professional help, the possible option of psychotropic medication, as well as information about alternative forms of treatment, such as psychotherapy, biofeedback, and yoga.

Following the main text, the resources section provides you with selected books and Web sites that can further help you in your quest for a better lifestyle.

Living in fear can be daunting, exhausting, frustrating, and disruptive. I know this to be true; I've struggled with fear myself. But I also know that it's very possible and probable that you will master your fears.

Let's begin our journey.

PART ONE

Understanding
Your Fears

1

Fear as a Way of Life

The only thing we have to fear is fear itself.

—FRANKLIN D. ROOSEVELT

IF SOMEONE COULD GIVE YOU A MAGIC PILL that would calm your fears, how would you live your life differently? If you weren't so worried about being careful and avoiding risks, what would you want to do? Whom would you want to meet? Where would you travel? What would you say to someone? How would you change? Who would you *be*?

The answers to these questions reveal what a fearful lifestyle is costing you. And they suggest how life could be different for you if you were more relaxed and confident instead of apprehensive and alarmed.

The Toll Fear Takes

I'm sure you know that fear is a problem for you (or for someone you love) because otherwise you wouldn't be reading this book. But you may not be aware of the many insidious ways in which fear has limited your ability to enjoy life, work creatively, and love freely.

Here are some of the problems of a fearful lifestyle that I often see in my work as a clinical psychologist.

A fearful lifestyle constricts thinking. Fear can limit your willingness

7

to even consider possibilities beyond a narrow, preconceived range of options.

- You may fall into a pattern of reflexive nay-saying.

- You may put enormous energy into finding fault with everything rather than weighing the relative merits or ascertaining the best course of action given the circumstances.

- You may exhaust yourself by worrying about every possible shortcoming, setback, pitfall, trouble, problem, or calamity that may result if you try something new.

- You may respond to people's suggestions and offers by letting your fear do the talking: "What, are you crazy?" or "How can you even *think* about that!"

A fearful lifestyle pinches choices. Fear can reduce the marvelous variety of options throughout life—the people you can meet, the careers you can pursue, the trips you can take, the fun you can have—and it leaves you with greatly reduced alternatives.

- You may feel hemmed in by the world rather than free to explore it.

- You may regard living as a burden, not an adventure.

- You may tell yourself, "There are so many terrible dangers out there" rather than, "There are so many amazing things to do."

- You may imagine that you have no choice but to live within your too-tight comfort zone, then complain, "I don't know what to do—I have so few options."

A fearful lifestyle restricts activities. Fear can prompt you to narrow the range of creative actions you're willing to take.

- You may avoid professional, social, or financial opportunities despite their overwhelming benefits.

- You may habitually turn down invitations or refuse to "go for it" rather than evaluate possibilities with an open mind.

- You may "put fear at the helm" and reject possible activities because "I'm uncomfortable with that" or because "I can't do that."

A fearful lifestyle can squeeze all the excitement, all the fun, and all the juiciness out of life. It's hard to enjoy yourself when so much of your energy is invested in fear.

- You may feel physically exhausted and emotionally depleted.

- You may find creative work difficult, even impossible.

- You may find friendship and love a source of fatigue rather than pleasure and sustenance.

- You may respond with gloom and dismay ("This is too stressful! I'm not used to this! I can't handle so much uncertainty!") instead of reacting to new experiences with joy and celebration ("Wow! This is fun! I love it! I'm so glad I tried that! What an experience!").

When fear restricts, constricts, pinches, and squeezes the freedom and delight out of your life, all that remains are the routine, mundane, dull, everyday situations—as well as the awful moments, the crises, and the tragedies that none of us can escape. But life doesn't have to be that way. It took many years for forty-three-year-old Ilana to understand that risks are an inevitable, essential part of life. That's when she realized that she was spending way too much time focusing on hazards and hardships to the exclusion of all the wonderful and enjoyable aspects of life. Life became "just one damn thing after another." Tossing out the lightness and delight of life, she staggered under the burden of I've-gotta-carry-this-load.

Safety First—Jake's Story

It took many years for Jake to understand that "safety first" isn't the best way to live. Currently in his early fifties, Jake had gone through a protracted phase of fearfulness during his late teens and twenties. Although gifted and well-trained as a classical guitarist, Jake felt uneasy about pursuing his musical career and hesitant about exploring other opportunities that were available to him. Fearing failure and rejection, he held back from embracing what life had to offer, both in personal and professional arenas.

He found work as a nurse-assistant on a hospital ward soon after turning twenty-two. Jake reasoned that this job would serve to support his "music habit," as he called it, much as other musicians, writers, and actors often work in restaurants or retail stores to support themselves. Friends and relatives often asked him why he'd work at a job so totally divorced from his artistic aspirations. He replied that he enjoyed working with patients, and the hospital job allowed him to pay the bills. However, Jake knew that even though he didn't like admitting it, working as a nurse-assistant also allowed him to avoid making tough decisions about his musical career. Fearing that he wouldn't be able to succeed as a classical guitarist, he put his dream on hold and let opportunities slip away.

Jake's shyness also impeded his ability to establish and nurture romantic relationships. Despite meeting interesting, attractive young women, he rarely dated. More motivated by fear than by passion, he shied away from taking risks. He couldn't believe that women really liked him despite the interest they showed. Ironically, when he did fall in love a few years later, his choice of partner was an emotionally distant, highly critical woman who confirmed his low opinion of himself and his suspicion that romance was unacceptably risky. (People with neurotic needs have an uncanny ability to attract each other—even across a crowded room.)

Years later, Jake recognized that he was being dragged down by his fear of change—and his fear of his own potential. If only he'd known then what he knows now. But, to paraphrase the Danish philosopher Søren Kierkegaard, life must be lived forward, but we understand it only by looking backward.

How Do You Do Fear?

Jake's story is just one instance of how a fearful lifestyle can limit an otherwise bright, energetic, capable person. If your fears are out of control, it's likely that you experience life as overwhelming and threatening—as one stressful, alarming event after another. However, even if your situation isn't that dramatic, apprehension and nervousness can take a toll on the quality and substance of your life. Living in fear doesn't necessarily mean you're terrified or incapable of functioning; indeed, the syndrome of fearful attitudes and behaviors is usually far more subtle. There are complex gradations of fear and many different ways that people express fear. Here are some of the most common:

- By isolating themselves
- By being overly compliant toward others
- By being hypervigilant
- By feeling numb
- By avoiding intimacy
- By avoiding rejection or disapproval
- By being overly controlling
- By refusing to respond at all to the situation they face
- By developing what psychologists call *reaction formation*—behaving in the opposite way from what you're feeling, such as acting macho or being disdainful or indifferent to your own fear

Fear may also be masked as an intense need for safety, or you may feel fear in the guise of doubt, indecisiveness, uncertainty, worry, or rigidity. Or you may feel little fear in the physical arena ("There's nothing I can't do") but gripping fear in the emotional arena ("I'm afraid of being alone" or "I'm terrified about what others think of me").

These consequences of a fearful lifestyle usually are expressed in a great variety of combinations, and the cumulative effect on any one person can range from mild discomfort to paralysis or panic.

A Way of Life, Not a Diagnosis

Before we proceed, I want to distinguish between excessive and inappropriate fear as a medical diagnosis and fear as an experiential approach to life. Many of us tend to think of *fear* as a type of mental illness—as phobias, panic reactions, anxiety reactions, and post-traumatic stress disorder (PTSD). Although these are valid disorders, I look at fear throughout this book from a nonmedical perspective—not as a *diagnosis* or an illness but as a *pattern of experience* that we have learned and that we can unlearn.

This book focuses on the whole person, not just a bundle of nervous symptoms. It pinpoints how to achieve the enriched life, rather than emphasizing the impaired life. The orientation is like the difference between approaching a weight problem with dieting versus developing a healthy way of eating. Dieting is a short-term solution with little chance of long-term success. By contrast, eating well is a long-term, quality-of-life, solution-oriented approach. My emphasis throughout this book moves away from a mental-illness model (what's wrong with you?) and toward mental well-being (what will enhance your life?).

But if, as I'm suggesting, a fearful lifestyle isn't necessarily a mental illness, how can it still cause so much damage to your life? And how does it develop? We'll examine these topics in more detail in chapter 3, but I'll touch on them briefly now.

A fearful lifestyle can develop in many ways, but one thing is always true. If you experience fear too frequently, too intensely, or for too long a duration—especially when you're young—you develop a state of mind that affects how you go about living in the world. Rather than fear being a response to a specific situation, fear becomes a way of life. What I'm describing is analogous to the difference between feeling angry in response to someone insulting you (an appropriate reaction to a specific situation) and becoming an angry person (a way of life). Or it's like the difference between feeling sad following a personal loss (an appropriate response to a specific situation) and becoming a melancholy person (a way of life).

When fear takes precedence in your life, your lifestyle is oriented to *accommodating* the fears, not *overcoming* them. You tend to watch out constantly for danger—danger on the job, danger at home, danger in your relationships, danger in the larger world. "Watching out" becomes a mentality in which your mind is always on the alert for danger. You are quick to respond with fear even in nonthreatening situations. You learn to avoid necessary risk, which prevents you from gaining experience that could be good for you in the long run. You develop an insatiable hunger for safety. In short, fear becomes a mind-set.

Although you may fantasize about a life that's safe, secure, and certain, these qualities in real life can only be relative. There is no absolute safety. Life is a risky business.

- By living, we risk dying.
- By loving, we risk losing.
- By feeling, we risk getting hurt.
- By learning, we risk feeling stupid.
- By trying, we risk failing.
- By speaking up, we risk being ridiculed.
- By succeeding, we risk reaching our limits.

Can you take steps to minimize these various risks? Of course. Will you ever eliminate *all* risk? Never.

How, then, do you live with these risks? How can you find ways to tame your fears, doubts, and uncertainties? These are the questions this book will answer.

Fear Is an Adaptive Response—*Sometimes*

How can you tell if your fear is *adaptive fear*, which helps keep you alive, alert, and appropriately cautious? How can you tell if your fear is *maladaptive fear*, which lacks any survival benefits and which makes life, work, and love difficult or (for some people) even impossible?

Here's a brief quiz that can help you answer these important questions.

IS YOUR FEAR ADAPTIVE OR MALADAPTIVE?

Answer true or false for each of the following statements as they generally describe your fears:

1. My fear usually assists me in coping with specific challenges, threats, and uncertainties.

2. My fear responds to a wider—and sometimes limitless—array of situations that may or may not be threatening or dangerous.

3. My fear is in proportion to the nature of the challenge, threat, or uncertainty I'm facing.

4. My fear is disproportionate to the nature of the challenge, threat, or uncertainty I'm facing.

5. My fear is relatively time-limited; it increases at a time of danger, then subsides.

6. My fear tends to be open-ended in time as well as focus; at times it may even be a continuous, generalized state of mind.

7. My fear ends with a sense of relief when I successfully decrease or eliminate the source of the fear.

8. My fear lingers even when the source of fear diminishes or ends.

9. My fear varies according to the severity of the threat.

10. My fear doesn't necessarily vary in proportion to the greater or lesser degree of danger.

To score your quiz, total the number of true answers for the odd-numbered statements; now total the true answers for the even-numbered statements. All of the odd-numbered statements describe reactions that can be characterized as adaptive fear. All of the even-numbered statements describe reactions that can be characterized as maladaptive fear.

If you have more true answers for odd-numbered statements than for even-numbered statements, your fear is more adaptive than maladaptive. Adaptive fear is an emotion that has saved the lives of countless men, women, and children in difficult situations. It is often necessary and appropriate; it warns us of real dangers. If you scored high for adaptive fear, congratulations. Your fear is working in your favor.

If you have more true answers for even-numbered than for odd-numbered statements, your fear is more maladaptive than adaptive, and you have some work to do. Fear should kick in when you need it but shouldn't control you when it's not useful or protective.

Adaptive fear is a nuanced emotion that diminishes during times of relative safety, while maladaptive fear lurks beneath the surface all the time, quick to make its presence known whenever there is discomfort, the unknown, or change.

Now that we've considered how fear can disrupt your life, let's have a look at the different ways that people express their fearfulness.

2

The Five Fear Styles

PEOPLE EXPRESS FEAR IN MANY DIFFERENT WAYS. Not only does the content of *what* people fear vary enormously; so does the style of *how* people express their fear. Many of us are aware, for instance, that there's often a difference between how men and women express fear. Starting in early childhood, girls have more role models for expressing fear, both in real life and in books, television shows, and movies. Many girls, and also some boys, are trained to be careful, afraid, even timid. Some receive parental and societal messages that promote or even reward fear. It's more socially acceptable for women to both admit to feeling fearful and to express fear directly. For some people, it's not only acceptable, it's almost demanded. "Whenever I went anywhere as a teenager," a friend told me, "my mother's parting words were, 'Be careful.' It made no difference whether I was going to school, on a date, or to visit my friends. Yet to my younger brother, she wouldn't say, 'Be careful,' she'd say, 'Stay out of trouble.' If he got into trouble, my parents would be mildly annoyed, but they'd respond with some casual retort, like 'Oh well, boys will be boys.' But if I got into trouble, they'd say, 'We *told* you to be careful!' There'd be panic, even hysteria, in their voices: 'You could have been kidnapped, raped, or killed!"

Men feel fear, too, of course, but our society teaches them to downplay it, deny it, or lie about it. Men often manifest fear indirectly—by getting angry, getting drunk, becoming loners, or avoiding situations they don't know how to handle. Even a routine situation, such as having to rely on other people for information, may cause both fear and an insistence on denying the fear. (A joke that made the rounds on one of my e-mail lists: "Why did Moses wander in the desert for forty years?" Answer: "Because he wouldn't ask for directions.") Many men struggle with intense fears without recourse to discussing, expressing, or even acknowledging what concerns them. Despite the fact that men's fears are more hidden—or perhaps *because* of this—their fears often become deeper and more burdensome.

What would account for boys' and men's relatively greater reluctance to acknowledge or exhibit fear? By the time boys reach the age of five or six, most males have internalized the message that fear isn't "manly" and should be hidden or denied. Later, during the school years, the predominant culture in that setting prompts boys to mock, harass, or even physically punish other boys who express fear openly. A boy who doesn't suppress his fearfulness may be labeled a "wimp," a "fag," or a "pussy."

This results in men and women generally receiving far different messages about admitting fear and about what form such fear can take. However, the fundamental questions for this book aren't what men and women *generally* feel, but rather what you as an individual *specifically* feel. Do you feel that fear is damaging your ability to enjoy life and accomplish your goals? And what shape does fear take for you?

What's Your Fear Style?

Although fear begins as just another emotion, over time it can create a self-concept and a personality style. To help you better understand how you express fear, I've devised a set of quizzes that you can take and score. The results will give you a clearer sense of your fear style. Following the quizzes, I'll explain the five basic fear styles and how they can affect you.

Here's how to use these quizzes:

- On a scale of 1 ("Not me at all") to 5 ("That's me!"), rate yourself on each set of statements using the following guide:

Never	=	1 point
Rarely	=	2 points
Sometimes	=	3 points
Frequently	=	4 points
Always	=	5 points

- After completing the five quizzes, enter the total score for each quiz in the space provided.

- Rank your styles as follows: the highest total score indicates your primary fear style, the next highest score is your secondary style, and so on.

- The order in which you've ranked your scores provides an overview of the ways in which you experience fear.

Detailed discussions in later chapters of this book will help you gain a better understanding of your style.

QUIZ #1

1. Do you hesitate to leave your comfort zone, avoiding situations that might cause you stress or anxiety?

2. Do you have trouble initiating conversations or speaking up for yourself?

3. Does it take you a long time to warm up to others at social gatherings?

4. Are you aware of bodily sensations when you're in social situations, such as your heart racing or your stomach churning?

5. Do you prefer to remain silent rather than speak up with others?

6. Are you fearful about making a social faux pas?

7. Do you shy away from social activities, spending a lot of time with passive activities, such as reading, watching TV, or using the computer?

8. When conversing with others, do you lose your focus on the conversation because you're worrying about how others are perceiving you?

9. Do you hate to be the center of attention?

10. Do you feel uncomfortable when someone compliments you?

11. Do you tend to live in your head rather than in your body?

12. Do you often believe that you are "not enough" (good enough, smart enough, attractive enough, and so on)?

Total score: _____

Quiz #2

1. Do you often feel keyed up or on edge about things that are happening in your life?

2. Do other people sometimes describe you as "too intense"?

3. Do you find it difficult to relax, even if there's nothing you really need to take care of?

4. Do you find it difficult to fall asleep, stay asleep, or have a good night's sleep?

5. Do you get easily alarmed over a possible problem?

6. Do things often seem a bigger deal to you than to other people you know?

7. Have you gotten feedback from other people to "calm down" or "don't worry"?

8. Do you get nervous right away when something unexpected happens?

9. Do you use the phrase "oh my God!" a lot?

10. Do you often get upset when you hear the news, weather, or business reports?

11. Do you feel tension-related problems in your body, such as stomachaches, headaches, or shoulder aches?

12. Do you think that you are responsible for too many things?

Total score: _____

Quiz #3

1. Is it important to you that people like you or approve of you?

2. Do you have difficulty saying "no" to people if they ask you for something?

3. Do you tend to give other people's needs priority over your own?

4. Do you think more in terms of what you *should* be doing rather than what you *want* to be doing?

5. Do you get upset if someone is upset with you?

6. Do you seek approval, advice, or reassurance from others before you act on what you want to do?

7. Do you have difficulty making decisions on your own?

8. Are you easily influenced by others' opinions, changing your point of view when someone disagrees with you?

9. Are you easily intimidated by an angry voice or a disapproving look?

10. Are you hesitant in speaking up, fearful that someone may not agree or like what you are saying?

11. Do you try to suppress angry feelings so as not to make waves and to keep everything calm?

12. Do you often go along with what others want, then feel hurt or resentful afterward because your opinion didn't count?

Total score: _____

Quiz #4

1. Would people be surprised to find out about underlying fears you harbor?

2. Do you become irritable or argumentative with others as an escape from your own bad feelings?

3. Do others accuse you of being inflexible, having to have things your way?

4. Do you have trouble asking for directions, afraid that you may be perceived as incompetent?

5. Do you sometimes brag about not being afraid of anything?

6. Do you catch yourself being more rigid or resistant than you want to be?

7. Do you wish you could be less serious and have more joy in your life?

8. Do you sometimes think that beneath your anger, you store a lot of fear?

9. Do you tend to be sarcastic or ridicule people rather than speak directly with them about what's bothering you?

10. Do you protect yourself by acting as though the best defense is a good offense?

11. Do you regard other people's fears as indicating weakness or lack of character?

12. Do you view yourself as hard on the outside, soft on the inside?

Total score: _____

Quiz #5

1. Is your behavior driven by a lot of "have to's" and "shoulds"?

2. Do you pay a great deal of attention to details or rules that other people don't seem to pay much mind to?

3. Do you think of yourself as a perfectionist?

4. Do you tend to orchestrate other people's lives, making sure that everyone is doing things the way they are "supposed" to be done?

5. Do others accuse you of being too controlling?

6. Do you tend to get really upset if things are out of order?

7. Do you hate when something unpredictable happens?

8. Do you have difficulty letting go of critical thoughts?

9. Do you feel compelled to do things the "right" way or not do them at all?

10. Do you call yourself harsh names when you make a mistake or fail to achieve what you want to do?

11. Do you frequently get annoyed with others' behavior because they go against your expectations?

12. Do you have trouble being spontaneous or dealing with change?

Total score: _____

Ranking and Assessing the Quizzes

Now that you've completed the quizzes, enter the total score for each quiz in the spaces provided:

Score for Quiz #1—Shy fear style: _____

Score for Quiz #2—Hypervigilant fear style: _____

Score for Quiz #3—Compliant fear style: _____

Score for Quiz #4—Macho fear style: _____

Score for Quiz #5—Controlling fear style: _____

Now rank your fear styles. The highest total score makes that your primary fear style, the next highest score is your secondary style, and so on.

Highest-ranking fear style: _____

Second highest-ranking fear style: _____

Third highest-ranking fear style: _____

Fourth highest-ranking fear style: _____

Lowest-ranking fear style: _____

As you review your results, keep these things in mind:

- Remember that this exercise provides a general *overview* of your fear style; it is not a formal, empirical test. The goal here is to get a handle on how fear contributes to your personality style.

- All people who take these quizzes will score something on each one. The lowest possible score on any one quiz would be 12 points; the highest possible score would be 60. However, a score of 12 would be implausible, as it would mean that you're counterphobic, or tending to respond to situations without any fear. The ideal situation is to receive a score in the middle range

(20–40), which suggests relatively mild and appropriate fears toward the issues discussed.

- The outcome of the quizzes will indicate a pattern that explains how your fears are expressed—shyness, hypervigilance, compliance, and so forth. If you scored 41 on controlling, for example, but only 18 on shyness, the relative scores would indicate that you are much more fearful about losing control than about how you come across to other people. The chief significance of this exercise isn't any one score; rather, it's the rank ordering of the five quizzes.

The Five Fear Styles

Now that you know what fear style is predominant in your life, it's time to learn more about each specific personality type. Keep in mind that these fear styles aren't mutually exclusive entities; they share some important features, and it's possible for a person to score high on more than one style. Most fearful people do tend to have a predominant style, however, that influences them in physical, emotional, and intellectual ways. Also remember that the five fear styles I've described are *not* medical diagnoses. Rather, they are patterns of living. In order to learn how to overcome your fears, you'll benefit from knowing how and in what situations your fears are triggered.

The following is an overview of the five fear styles.

Shyness

People with this fear style tend to exhibit passive, inhibited, constrained behavior. The Shy person's often-repeated motto is "I don't feel safe or comfortable with other people." This fear is manifested with:

- A timid mind
- A silent voice

- Restricted actions
- A still body
- Reserved relationships

GERARD—A MAN OF FEW WORDS

Gerard, forty-four years old, is a computer programmer who has wrestled with shyness his entire life. His predominant fear is a fear of intimate encounters, both one on one and in larger gatherings. Although well aware of his recurrent struggle, Gerard still can't get past the many layers of doubt and self-consciousness that underlie his fear. "I know I need to put my fear aside in order to take action," he admits, "but I usually procrastinate or avoid situations altogether until dealing with them isn't an option." His battle with fear has contributed to many problems, including the collapse of his marriage and its painful aftermath. "After I got divorced, I sat home each evening after work and did nothing. It was stupid. I was lonely and alone but I felt too afraid to *do* anything about it. Instead, I'd just obsess about what went wrong, beat myself up, and imagine the awful things that everyone was saying about me."

Hypervigilance

This fear style shows up as nervous, agitated, overly responsive, and on edge. The Hypervigilant motto is "I feel keyed up and worried about so many things." This person expresses fear with:

- An alarmed mind
- A hysterical voice
- Agitated actions
- A hyperactive body
- Frenzied relationships

SHARON—NERVOUS AND UPTIGHT

Sharon, a thirty-eight-year-old mother and part-time social worker is highly attentive to everyone around her but takes this potential virtue to a fault. "I guess I assume responsibility for more things than I need to," Sharon admits, "but I'm afraid to let go of my concerns. I worry about what might happen if I do." For instance, she always picks up her children from school even though the kids are now twelve and ten, ages at which many other parents let their own children walk home alone or with their friends. Sharon's rationale: "Even though we live in a safe neighborhood, you can never be too careful. You never know what might happen. My husband says I'm overprotective and should let go a little. That's easy for him to say but not so easy for me to do." In addition, Sharon is often exhausted from rushing around, attending to real and imagined obligations. She herself is aware that she needs to calm down, take things at a slower pace, and let some events unfold without her constant efforts to manage them, but she finds easing up difficult, if not impossible. "I just don't know how to relax," she admits. "I have trouble falling asleep—I'm always thinking about problems that could arise and all the responsibilities I need to take care of."

Compliance

People who are Compliant are dependent, hesitant, wishy-washy, and easily intimidated. The Compliant person's typical proclamation is "I'm devastated if someone disapproves of me." This fear is expressed with:

- An unsure mind

- A hesitant voice

- Yielding actions

- A cautious body

- Deferential relationships

DORIS—A DUTIFUL DAUGHTER

Doris, a fifty-four-year-old homemaker, has been drowning in self-doubt all her life. In her family of origin, she was the stereotypical "good girl," always ready to please others and make her parents proud. Some aspects of her personality were a reasonable response to the family situation: Doris's father wasn't home much, and her mother had her hands full with a difficult younger child. "I knew that Mom needed me to take care of myself," Doris explains. "So, to get by, I pretended to be okay all the time—even when I felt frightened or angry or overwhelmed." Although her reaction was understandable, it still had problematic consequences. Doris feels that her legacy of living life as a pleaser is that "I'm not only worried about what other people think, I'm not even sure what *I* think. I'm scared to have my own opinion. I hesitate to make decisions. I work too hard to gain approval from others."

Machismo

By contrast, the Macho person is rigid and combative on the outside while apprehensive on the inside. Like the Cowardly Lion in *The Wizard of Oz*, the Macho person will roar to intimidate, showing fear only when someone stands up to him or her. The characteristic attitude is "I won't show anyone—including myself—that I'm afraid." This fear manifests with:

- An inflexible mind
- A harsh voice
- Oppositional actions
- A stiff body
- Unbending relationships

ROB—MACHO, MACHO MAN

Rob, a twenty-eight-year-old policeman, is a classic Macho person. Frequently described as "the cop who ain't afraid of *nothing*," he's proud of his reputation and considers it a personal and professional asset. "Nobody messes with me," boasts Rob. "If they do, they wish they hadn't." At the same time, he admits privately that his macho image bears no resemblance to what he feels like inside. "In reality, I'm afraid a lot of the time. I wish I was just as fearless as people think I am, but mostly I avoid the fear, doing it as easily as a cheat deals from the bottom of the deck. From the time I was a kid, I learned to keep my fears well hidden. I grew up in a tough neighborhood where you learned to 'take it like a man.' It didn't matter if your heart was pounding or your nerves were stretched to the breaking point. The worst thing you could be was a coward."

The Controller

Finally, the Controlling person is compulsive, compelled, critical, and driven. "It drives me crazy if things aren't done the way they should be done" is the Controlling motto. Maintaining a strict sense of order minimizes surprise, which, in turn minimizes fear. Other attributes include:

- A critical mind

- A demanding voice

- Driven actions

- An intense body

- Domineering relationships

JANICE—BECAUSE I SAID SO

Janice, who's thirty-four, single, and a public relations executive, is an archetypal Controlling person. She prides herself on her professional accomplishments and works long hours, often well into the night. Janice doesn't just push herself, however; she pushes everyone around her as well. Her subordinates (and even her colleagues) regard her as a stern taskmaster. Her controlling attitude has damaged more than her work relationships; this tendency to dominate others has ruined her love life as well. "When my boyfriend dumped me last year," Janice explains, "he said he couldn't stand my criticizing and controlling him any more. I was taken completely by surprise. I thought he wasn't good enough for me—and then *he* dumped *me*. I couldn't believe it!" The shock of this loss prompted Janice to enter group therapy. To her dismay, she received feedback that confirmed her boyfriend's perception of her as a control freak. Janice attempted to defend herself: "People don't understand that I have a lot of fears. Unless things are done exactly as I think they ought to be done, I feel helpless and overwhelmed. Being in control makes me feel more secure. But now that I'm living alone, I'm miserable. It sounds awful to say, but without someone to control, my life seems worthless."

Fear—A Pattern You Can Change

To live with fear and not be afraid is the final test of maturity.

—Edward Weeks

Now that you've identified your dominant fear style or styles, you've already taken a big step—acknowledging your attitudes and patterns of behavior in a clear light. What's next?

The next step is developing skills that will release you from fear's constraints. Give yourself a big hand. You're on the way to learning how to live a freer, more adventurous life.

First, though, let's consider how a fearful lifestyle begins.

3

How a Fearful Lifestyle Develops

Sid, the only child of Holocaust survivors, grew up in a household haunted by unfathomable loss and grief. He has struggled with intense fearfulness since his boyhood years.

Allan's father died shortly after the boy's thirteenth birthday; in the fifteen years since then, Allan has felt unsure of himself, concerned about his safety in the world, and tense about whatever negative surprises may happen next.

Joanna was a nervous and shy child. Now a young adult, she has continued to feel overwhelmed and alarmed by many aspects of everyday life.

AS THESE STORIES SUGGEST, a fearful lifestyle can arise from a multitude of sources. Sometimes the source is an obvious, glaring situation, such as when a child is injured, traumatized, abused, or neglected. At other times fearfulness arrives by another route: physical or emotional illness, parents' financial hardship, or the loss of a close relationship through death or divorce. An inborn temperament, too, can intensify environmental circumstances.

My primary intention in writing this book is to offer ways to change a fearful lifestyle. But to understand the way out of fearfulness, it's also important to understand the way in.

The Origins of a Fearful Lifestyle

There's no single cause for a fearful lifestyle. In fact, several kinds of factors—even diametrically opposite factors—can contribute strongly to creating a fearful personality. Here are the most important determinants.

Antecedents from Childhood: Loss and Trauma

Of the many factors that can contribute to a fearful lifestyle, the most powerful is tragic or traumatic life experiences. Physical and emotional trauma can significantly damage a person's sense of the world as a safe place. One of the legacies of such events is persistent fear that the loss will happen again. You may automatically play it safe, not wishing to tempt fate. This loss of innocence can be especially severe if the trauma occurs early in life. There doesn't have to be an abundance of trauma; even a single event can have striking consequences.

Too Much Too Soon—Catherine's Story

Catherine, currently thirty-eight years old, had an easy childhood until she turned fourteen. Much to everyone's shock, her mother was diagnosed with stage-four cancer and died three months later. This trauma hit the whole family with devastating force. Catherine's father couldn't manage doing double duty as a parent. He deteriorated emotionally, resorting to alcohol to assuage his grief. Since her father was barely able to function as a breadwinner and a parent, Catherine found herself in a position of being the unofficial head of the household. She not only acquired the roles of cook and housekeeper, she also carried the burden of mothering her sister, Alicia, who was barely twelve at the time. Catherine coped with the situation by growing hypercompetent and rigid about her heavy domestic responsibilities.

Now, more than twenty years later, Catherine lives in a state of high anxiety that manifests itself primarily as a need for control. Even the slightest degree of uncertainty causes her to worry that events will "go bad." Unfortunately, Catherine's rigidity and pessimism often contribute precisely to the bad outcomes she fears. She has alienated friends and relatives, developed a reputation as a control freak among her business associates, and harmed her marriage by always insisting that everything goes her way.

As Catherine's story indicates, traumatic events can dramatically change the carefree, innocent days of childhood into the burdensome, worried days of adulthood. Kids who assume an adult role prematurely often perform the tasks well enough from an outside perspective; inside, however, the child is often filled with psychic turmoil. The child may worry and ask herself, "Am I doing a good enough job?" The child may feel angry, wondering, "How did I get stuck with this?" or "Why can't Dad [or Mom] be the parent?" The child may feel alone and lonely, feeling that she has to take care of her family even though nobody takes care of *her*. Finally, the child may feel resentment: "Why did Mom have to die?"

Trauma can occur within a range of severity. Some events are clearly devastating, such as what Catherine experienced. Other occurrences, such as the peaceful death of a grandparent, may strike one person as traumatic while leaving another within the same family relatively unaffected. Events that aren't terrible by adult standards may nonetheless throw a child off-balance, take him by surprise, or leave him unsure of how to cope. One such event might be a close friend suddenly moving away. World events such as the September 11 attacks may not directly affect the child, yet they can still become a defining moment in the child's life, with aftereffects of recurrent, distressing worries, terrifying images, and nightmares. As one child told me, "I can't stop thinking about those planes going into the buildings. I live in Oregon, but I still keep feeling so bad about kids my age whose parents died. I keep thinking about what would happen to me if my mom or dad died."

Does more trauma in your life mean that your lifestyle will be more fearful? Not necessarily. Some people who have experienced a lot of trauma manage to stay resilient and open to life's challenges and adventures despite tragic loss. Yet trauma can certainly be a major contributor to a fearful lifestyle.

Subtle Trauma: No Words for What Happened

Other people grow fearful as a result of secret, quiet trauma that children can't reveal to anyone—trauma that leaves them dealing with their situation by themselves. One of the most fear-inducing situations for children is not understanding what's happening and having no one to turn to for explanation, advice, or comfort. Kids have little comprehension of the significance of many situations, so they naturally look to other people for clues to help them make sense of their world. But the information they obtain from others may be baffling, dishonest, evasive, or even totally confusing.

WHAT'S GOING ON?—JOEY'S STORY

To the outside world, Joey had a wonderful, loving, attentive mother. Yet Joey found his relationship with his mother both baffling and horrifying. For many years, his mother would behave differently with the boy in public than in private. She was cordial, warm, and maternal when others were around but inappropriate, seductive, and controlling when alone with him. Joey often heard from family friends that his mother was wonderful, yet his experience of her terrified him. He never knew from one day to the next what her mood would be. She gave him the creeps, yet he couldn't describe why. At the same time, he needed her and he wanted her love. But she was so unpredictable. Only years later, when Joey had grown up, did he realize that his mother suffered from bipolar disorder and was also a closet alcoholic. That realization explained a lot, but he'd had no way of understanding the situation when he was a child.

As a rule, children don't know how to describe what's wrong in a situation, and they often feel, and truly are, at the mercy of powerful people in their lives. As a result, they do what they need to do to survive in their family of origin, becoming quiet or sad, loud-mouthed or intimidated, compliant or defiant. As adults, many people continue to live their lives in the same manner, even when they aren't living under the same circumstances. Their fearful lifestyle has become so familiar to them that it continues, even when it no longer serves any survival benefit.

Temperament and Genetics

Another major contributing factor to a fearful lifestyle is temperament and genetic makeup. Temperament is one of the most powerful determinants of personality. Even as newborns, babies aren't the "blank slates" that some people tend to consider them. Some babies are serene, some nervous, some highly alert; some are easily reassured when uncomfortable while others are difficult to calm; some are eager to be held, while others shy away from human contact.

Jake, whose story I related in chapter 1, is an example of the influence of temperament. His family of origin was generally happy, and Jake had grown up feeling appreciated and loved by both his parents. He hadn't suffered any significant losses during childhood or adolescence. However, Jake was temperamentally high-strung and sensitive. As he entered adolescence, he found dealing with life more difficult rather than easier. He felt hesitant or alarmed about many situations that other people would take in stride. Shy among most people, self-effacing to an extreme, he found many ordinary events overwhelming. Jake's experience shows the effects of a fearful temperament plus overprotective parents, a separate issue we'll explore now.

Parental Extremes—Over- and Underprotectiveness

No study has shown that one particular parental style works best. However, extremes in parental styles and strategies do create problems. Some parents are overprotective, and won't let their child be. Other parents are so distant that they leave their child vulnerable to physical or emotional harm. Both parenting styles can create similar results.

OVERPROTECTIVENESS

Kids know intuitively that they will never get what they want from life without taking some risks. The truth is, the benefits of risk can be enormous. When parents strive to create a risk-free life for their kids, the effort may be well intentioned but is ultimately counterproductive.

Occasional experiences of parental overprotectiveness won't create a fearful lifestyle. However, recurrent experiences can provide an inadvertent message that many or most situations are dangerous and that the child isn't capable of dealing with troubling occurrences on his or her own but must rely on parents' intervention and protection to be safe in the world.

The following are some of the negative side effects of parents' cumulative overprotectiveness:

- *Overprotectiveness creates a false sense of security.* Kids in this situation tend to assume that Mommy and Daddy will always be there, and they develop an exaggerated sense of their parents' omnipotence. The result is often shock and dismay when difficult, frustrating, or painful experiences happen anyway, as is inevitable.

- *Overprotectiveness deprives children of the necessary experiences of dealing with their mistakes and errors of judgment.* If the parent steps in to protect the child from all difficulties and mistakes, the child won't learn the consequences of his or her actions. The child will assume that Mom and Dad will hold a safety net no matter what he or she does. A failure-free or frustration-free environment causes more problems than it solves.

- *Overprotectiveness deprives children of the opportunity to assess risks, handle challenging situations, learn coping skills, and develop confidence.* Very young children benefit from clear-cut messages about danger. Kids younger than five or six can't make subtle distinctions about risk, and they aren't capable of abstract thinking. From about the ages of seven or eight, however, children need experience in assessing risks. They need to see gradations of danger and learn to make more subtle decisions about their responses. Many parents thwart this process by presenting only all-or-nothing statements (this is safe, that is dangerous) about the world.

- *Overprotectiveness deprives children of realistic role models.* If parents can honestly assess their own lives, most would admit that they've learned a lot because they took risks even when things didn't work out just right. They've gained knowledge, even wisdom, about calculating costs and benefits. They've learned to obtain more information before taking a big gamble. They've developed an ability to balance a need for excitement with a need for safety. Yet these same people often limit their own kids' efforts to undergo the same process and gain the same wisdom.

When overprotectiveness leads to fear, it's not because the parents have been negligent or unconcerned. On the contrary, this process occurs because parents are too concerned or too worried. Some parents claim that when raising kids, you can never be too careful. Ironically, being too careful can be risky in its own right, helping to foster children's inability to cope.

UNDERPROTECTIVENESS

The flip side of this is parental underprotectiveness. Too little protection, like too much, can foster a climate of fear.

Consider Catherine's story. After her mother's death and her father's alcoholism, Catherine and her sister ended up largely fending for themselves. Catherine, especially, carried a load of responsibility far too heavy for a fourteen-year-old. Many children in such pseudoparental roles suffer similar side effects as they struggle with duties beyond their coping skills. Even when they manage remarkably well, assuming adult roles while still a child will always take a psychic toll.

- *Underprotectiveness creates a basic sense of mistrust about the world.* Children who aren't well cared for (either physically or emotionally) rarely feel safe or secure in their environment.

- *Underprotectiveness creates dangerous situations, for children can't possibly know how to cope with all the problems and risks in life.* This situation puts kids at risk both inside the home and elsewhere. When they're on their own and have no one to turn to, children often get into trouble with high-risk activities.

- *Underprotectiveness often prompts children to worry that they aren't doing a good enough job.* They may develop what is called the "impostor syndrome," feeling that although in reality they're coping well, someone will discover how little they actually know or how insecure they actually feel.

- *Underprotectiveness leaves children without adequate role models.* This situation not only subjects kids to unreasonable expectations and tasks but also leaves them to tackle their responsibilities and problems without guidance.

Since so much of what underprotected children deal with has been fraught with risk, the result may be long-lasting fear of what others consider ordinary life events. Insufficiently protected by their parents, they may grow into adults who wait in perpetual fear of the next crisis, the next setback, the next calamity. Alternatively, they may take on the Macho fear style, with bravado on the outside masking fear on the inside (e.g., people who seek out hazardous activities or engage in high-risk sexual relationships).

Where's the Happy Medium?

How can parents respond to their children in ways that are neither excessive nor inadequate? Social psychologist Stanley Schacter's research indicates that when people are in an ambiguous or potentially threatening situation, they observe or communicate with one another to determine what emotions they should feel. In addition, they seek knowledge of others' emotional states to help them decipher their own. Schacter's work is relevant to our discussion because it helps us understand how children learn ways of responding to frightening situations. If your parents' reactions were extreme, their responses undoubtedly fostered apprehension in you.

Here's a scenario that shows how three different parental responses can influence children's emotional outlooks.

Imagine a routine mishap during early childhood. A toddler, still unsteady on his feet, is curious to explore his world. Attracted by a sparkling new toy, he runs, loses his balance, and hits his head on the playroom floor. Startled, he looks at his mother to determine what has happened.

In scenario 1, Mother is terrified. She panics, shouting hysterically, "Oh my God!" The child bursts into tears, convinced that something terrible has occurred. If scenarios such as this one take place *frequently* over the years, the scene is set for the child to develop a fearful lifestyle and become timid, hypervigilant, needy, rigid, or compulsive. When a parent is overly reactive, it tends to intensify a child's natural fear.

Scenario 2 shows the opposite reaction. When the toddler falls, Mother is either unavailable or else physically present but emotionally unresponsive. The child, startled, senses no concern or reassurance from his parent, which heightens his anxiety. Or, turning to his mother for comfort, he gets scolded instead: "Oh, stop being such a crybaby—you didn't hurt yourself." Either way, the child receives none of the nurturing that would allay his fears.

By contrast, scenario 3 presents a mother who is calm but concerned. She checks the child out, reassures him, kisses the boo-boo, and tells him that everything is okay. The child's fear is eased. He continues his exploration. Through this even-tempered response, families create an encouraging place for a child to grow, take risks, and learn when it's appropriate to be fearful and when it's not. Safe families accept mistakes and respect self-determination.

The best parenting style encourages a child's confidence and respects his feelings while still teaching him about how to respond to life's dangers. Scary stories as well as emotional hovering are poor foundations for building confidence.

EXERCISE: WHAT HAPPENED IN YOUR FAMILY?

1. Which type of these scenarios do you believe happened most frequently in your family? _____

   _____

2. How do you think you were affected as a child by the scenarios you experienced? _____

   _____

3. Do you think you continue to be affected by these childhood experiences?_____

   _____

4. If so, how? _____

   _____

Parental Expectations

Another significant influence in fostering a fearful lifestyle is unrealistic expectations, either too high or too low.

Let's say that your parents expected you to be perfect, tolerating no errors of judgment, no goofs, no blunders, no carelessness, no laziness. You, being a normal kid, invariably messed up, misconstrued situations, misunderstood requests, or simply felt lazy or unmotivated at times. Yet your parents' high expectations may have left you feeling guilty about your behavior, even though your behavior was entirely age-appropriate. This situation can give rise to an anxious state of mind, as you may have worried intensely about "letting your parents down" even when you hadn't.

Mike, a ten-year-old boy I've counseled, has expressed great anxiety about his grades. Although worrying about grades is a natural concern, Mike felt such disproportionate fear about doing well that I decided to explore the matter further.

"What would it mean if you do get a bad grade?" I asked him during a session.

"It would mean I'm not doing as well as I could be," he replied, dejectedly.

"And if you don't do as well in school as you could?"

"I won't get into a top college."

I decided to follow what now appeared to be a strand of fear to its source. "And what happens if you don't get into a top college?"

"I won't be able to provide for my family."

"And then?"

Mike looked distraught. "Well—they won't have good food to eat or a good house to live in, and they won't be able to go on nice vacations, and *it'll be all my fault!*"

At age ten, this boy was already worried that he'd be a failure in life. Is it because Mike himself created this whole good provider–trophy home–top vacation scenario? No, I don't believe that. I couldn't help but hear Mom and Dad's voices and their expectations speaking through their son.

Gina's story is quite different. This thirteen-years-old's parents have few expectations of her. They show little interest in her accomplishments at school, express few concerns about her social life, and exhibit little curiosity about her in other ways. Both parents are thoroughly wrapped up in their own careers and spend little time with their only child. Gina says, "My parents aren't there for me," and she's right. She receives so little guidance that she's often adrift, unsure of what anyone wants of her and confused about what she should be doing. The result for such a young adolescent isn't a feeling of freedom; it's pervasive anxiety.

Gina's parents are, in fact, negligent toward their daughter. However, even parents who are somewhat more attentive to their children than Gina's may also burden their kids with insufficient expectations. Some parents I know boast that they trust their kids so fully that they make few or no demands on them; they *know* that their children will never make any serious mistakes, do something mischievous, or fall short in any way. This attitude is short-sighted. Kids (even little lawyers with big mouths) need clear, age-appropriate limits and boundaries. The absence of clear, thoughtful expectations is a burden, not a gift.

The Family "Atmos-Fear"

Kids are generally more sensitive and more intuitive than most parents give them credit for. Their emotional antennae are remarkably sensitive to the moods within a family. They easily pick up signals of fear, even when they can't identify its source or understand what's happening. Kids are excellent observers but poor interpreters of events. They'll notice changes, such as "Dad isn't home as much as he used to be," or "Mom is angry a lot." For this reason, parents need to help children interpret events in an age-appropriate way.

Parental Responses to World Events

In addition to family trauma, events and crises in the outside world can affect a child's emotional responses. Just as John F. Kennedy's assassination was a defining event for a previous generation, the events of September 11 will be the defining event for children in the current generation. With today's graphic media coverage, other national and international events—the war in Iraq, earthquakes, floods, plane crashes, abductions, and so forth—can also prompt fearfulness in kids, even when these calamities take place thousands of miles away. Children's reactions to these events will differ, depending in part on the kids' own sensitivities and their parents' responses. Consider three scenarios of how parents responded to the September 11 attacks and terror-related incidents in the years afterward.

In scenario 1, Father responds by becoming hysterical in full view of his children: "Oh my God, what's going to happen next! We'll never be safe again! These terrorists are *everywhere!*" His children, seeing their father distraught, lack information but are well aware of his intense emotion, which troubles and frightens them without fostering any abilities to cope.

Scenario 2 isn't alarmist, but it's problematic for another reason: it resorts to minimizing the situation. Following a recent terrorist alert, Dad, seeking to protect his school-age children, acts as if nothing significant is occurring. "Oh, don't worry about it. These alerts mean nothing," he tells them following news of a national upgrade to Code Orange. By minimizing the situation, he deprives his kids of any chance to understand what is happening and any opportunity to learn how to cope well with stressful situations.

Scenario 3 offers a better response. Dad feels intense fear, but he chooses to express his fear only in adult company—with his wife, relatives, and friends—who then share their own worries with him. When speaking to his school-age children, however, he offers a more measured response. He explains the terror alert system to his kids in age-appropriate language. He lets the children ask questions, and he answers them honestly but without a contagious sense of panic. Dad explains that the actual terror attacks have been extraordinary events, that the new terror alert system will hopefully prevent further attacks, and that the children's immediate environment is safe. This results in the children learning that it's acceptable to be afraid, but that you can keep the fear contained; it doesn't have to take over your life.

If parents allow a constant procession of tragic and horrific images to enter the family home, kids will have difficulty dealing with so much fearful stimuli. Naomi's parents avoided creating that burden for their daughter. Following the World Trade Center attacks, they limited her exposure to TV and newspapers. They knew they did the right thing when Naomi told friends, "I was scared, but my parents seemed okay, so I guess I'm okay, too."

Current Relationships: Helpful or Harmful?

Early experiences do indeed have a huge influence on our emotional development and our responses to the world. However, childhood experiences aren't the whole story. Because you are a work in progress, later events in life can also have profound influence. Love relationships can be especially crucial in this regard, with either positive or negative results.

Some relationships offer hope and promise, thus decreasing tension and anxiety while providing nurturance and support. Think of an adult relationship—perhaps with a friend, a relative, a spouse, a therapist, or a lover—that made you feel really good about yourself. If so, did it:

- Foster more self-confidence?

- Make you feel more hopeful?

- Improve your ability to deal with specific challenges?

- Encourage you to speak up?

- Prompt you to take action?

- Help you develop insight and courage?

- Inspire a greater sense of safety?

- Help you appreciate who you are and what you have to offer?

- Diminish your fears both in intensity and frequency?

On the other hand, some relationships *betray* hope and promise, thereby *increasing* long-standing fears as a result of criticism, intimidation, confusion, and ambiguity. Have you experienced this sort of relationship? If so, did you find that it:

- Diminished your self-confidence?

- Discouraged you from speaking up?

- Prompted you to hold back from taking action?

- Kept you in old patterns of hostility, inadequacy, or abuse?

- Reinforced patterns of fear, uncertainty, and self-doubt?

- Intensified a sense of dependency and neediness?
- Kept old wounds from healing?
- Left you feeling pessimistic about what you have to offer?
- Intensified your fears about the present and the future?

Now that you understand how a fearful lifestyle develops, it's time to move on to learning new skills that will help you break the pattern. This is what the rest of this book will address.

4

Understanding the Change Process

YOU NOW UNDERSTAND more about how you've become so fearful. You've been living this way for a long time, but now you're ready— or at least getting ready—to change.

How can you make those changes happen? How can you learn the necessary skills to make a better life for yourself?

Perhaps you've fantasized about how great it would be if you could just snap your fingers and change *just like that*. Some people talk as though that's how change happens. I'm sure you've encountered friends, family members, coworkers, and even total strangers who believe that you can put fear aside simply by force of will. Maybe some of those people have told you, "There's nothing to be afraid of," "Don't be scared," "Don't be so shy," "Don't worry so much," "Make up your mind," or similar proclamations. You and I know it's not that easy.

What You Need to Know about Change

One doesn't discover new lands without consenting to lose sight of the shore for a very long time.

—ANDRÉ GIDE

Just being told to change or wanting to change isn't how it happens. Change is a process, not an instantaneous event. Time will change you. Life circumstances will change you. Choices you make will change you. But you don't want simply to wait for those events to happen. You want to be proactive and make the change happen. In addition, you definitely want to avoid changing in the opposite direction—becoming ever more fearful or creating an even more restricted life for yourself.

As you consciously begin to change, it will be helpful for you to appreciate the following concepts:

- *Change is inevitable.* Trying to stop change would be like trying to stop a river from flowing. It's not possible. No matter how much energy you expend in this effort, the river's force is stronger than you are. So why not have an open mind and welcome change instead of automatically resisting it?

- *Change isn't always difficult or troublesome.* Some change is actually easy and pleasant, so don't panic the moment you hear that change is on the horizon. As you become more comfortable with change, you'll trust that no matter what changes you need to make or how resistant you are initially to a new situation, you'll eventually come to terms with what you need to face.

- *Change may actually make your life a lot more comfortable and pleasant after you adapt to it.* Some examples are learning how to use the computer, letting go of your resistance to exercise, and easing up on your need to control a relationship. Indeed, don't be surprised if some of the changes you fight tooth and nail become aspects of your life that you'll most embrace.

- *Your resistance to change is often a struggle between opposing factors of your own personality.* It's not unusual if a part of you (the risk-taking part) wants to experience life in all its infinite variety while another part of you (the cautious part) craves nothing more than to be out of harm's way. For change to happen, you must find a way for these two parts of yourself to live together in harmony.

- *Fear of change is usually fear of the unknown.* As you get to know more about what you're up against and what or who can help you deal with it, most situations become less frightening.

- *Change is generally easier if you cope with it in stages.* Although some major changes in life may be thrust upon you without warning, it helps at such times to encounter change by means of a sequence of steps. You don't have to cope with everything all at once. You can move at your own pace to assimilate new realities. Give yourself the time you need to allow new ways to become more familiar and comfortable.

So the question isn't really *whether* you'll change, but rather *how much* and *in what ways*. Will you change without awareness or volition—just letting change happen without clarity of mind or choice? Or will you evaluate and embrace change with your eyes wide open?

Approaching Change with a Good Attitude

To conquer fear is the beginning of wisdom.

—BERTRAND RUSSELL

As with any change you wish to accomplish—whether it's a matter of learning to cultivate confidence or learning to make better decisions—there are three prerequisites for mastering your fears.

1. Acknowledge Fear as a Core Attitude

To work toward meaningful change, you have to be honest with yourself. You must give up blaming others for your troubles. You need to stop justifying your fears, believing that there's no other choice except to live in fear. You need to admit that chronic worrying, pessimistic beliefs, obsessive thinking, paralyzing indecisiveness, and a perpetual need for control are symptoms of maladaptive fear. Acknowledging the problem allows you to recognize how fear limits your options, drains your energy, and thwarts your ability to grow.

2. Realize That You Can Change

Most people dislike leading anxious, fear-burdened lives, but they may feel that they have no choice. If you fall into this category, you may believe that your fear-prone personality is just "how you are" and that you can't do anything about it. I recommend that you perceive fearfulness not as a fixed trait, but as an attitude, an inclination, a disposition, a pattern of living that you can change. Just as you can acquire other physical, intellectual, and emotional skills—from curbing your temper to learning managerial techniques—you can acquire skills that help you remain calm and develop your courage. Much of this book focuses on teaching you these skills.

Believing that you can change your pattern of living means that you're no longer relying on magical or wishful thinking—"If only my life were different," "If only I were a natural-born risk-taker," "Where's my knight in shining armor?"—and puts you in the driver's seat.

3. Embrace Change

Finally, getting ready for change includes a decision to *embrace* change. You've been living fearfully; now it's time to explore another way to live. Now it's time to move from hopelessness ("This is the way I am; I can't change or even adapt, alter, or diminish my responses") to hopefulness ("I am a growing, dynamic, intelligent person who doesn't have to stay stuck; I can modify, revise, and change my fear response"). It's time to move from focusing on your weaknesses ("I can't do this") to focusing on your strengths ("I'm good at this").

Like many new things, the skills you'll learn in the following chapters will take a while to understand, implement, and master. It takes time to grasp new concepts and develop new skills. It also takes time to appreciate how acquiring these skills will help you change your life. Be patient and have faith that you'll get to where you want to be.

Difficulties on the
Road to Change

This isn't to say that you'll arrive without encountering some ups and downs along the way. Forewarned is forearmed. Here are some typical difficulties you may confront.

Riding a Bumpy Road

No matter how much you say you're motivated to change, you can count on your fears to ambush you. You may feel ambivalent not only about the effort required to change, you may even feel ambivalent about the desire to feel less fearful. Why? Because what you want consciously may not be the primary agenda for your unconscious. There may be a part of you that *doesn't* want to be grown up and have to deal with scary situations, risks, and uncertainties. Maybe you just want to be taken care of or wish for gain without pain, safety without risk, and change without effort.

Sometimes your motivation for pursuing the change process wavers. You may feel as if you're stuck with the same old problems in the same old ways. You may feel restless, annoyed, or impatient with yourself or other people. You may feel calm and wonderful one week, then confused the next about whether you're making any progress at all. You may get sidetracked. You may feel that the road is too bumpy or aimless, or that you've reached a plateau and can't go any further. Rest easy. Change is complex, and it's not at all uncommon for people to feel that their progress isn't steady or smooth. In fact, the path to change is uneven and rough more often than not. Setbacks do occur, but they don't mean you've been knocked all the way back to square one, only that you have to get back on track and persevere. Trust the process. Be patient. Change almost always occurs as a gradual series of small steps, not one big dramatic event that happens all at once and changes you once and for all.

Frustration, confusion, and ambivalence are normal. Don't let them stop you from moving ahead.

Unlearning What You've Already Learned

> *Fears are educated into us and can, if we wish, be educated out.*
>
> —KARL MENNINGER, M.D.

Unless you were born yesterday, you'll most likely have to unlearn some things you've already learned. This is true for big things, such as unlearning a well-conditioned fear response, and it's true for little things too, such as trying a new food rather than automatically saying no to it. You may hesitate to modify your customary ways of thinking. You may shy away from the need to change any behavior that's entrenched in your personality. Yet deep down you know that if you keep doing the same thing in the same way, you'll end up in the same place. And you really don't want to remain stuck in fear, do you?

Remember, you don't have to *like* unlearning old ways; you just have to do it. Why? Because frequently that's the only way to change.

Worrying about "Pockets of Ignorance"

Perhaps your fear of change is based on a worry that new situations will expose your ignorance to others. With new people, new activities, or new conversations, you may be afraid that you'll be in over your head and that others will discover how inept or incompetent you really are.

Over the years I've noticed that everyone—and I mean everyone—has what I call "pockets of ignorance." It's as though you were absent for a week during ninth grade and somehow you never picked up a bit of knowledge that was part of the curriculum that week. Or you took a wilderness vacation for a week and missed the front-page news; now you don't know what everyone else seems to know. Perhaps you never learned what the word "paradoxical" means. Or you don't know who Luciano Pavarotti is. Or you never learned how to program a VCR. Or perhaps you don't even know what you don't know until other people start chatting away about something and you feel so out of touch. And now you're embarrassed that others will find out, so you shy away from certain situations or conversations. Eventually avoidance becomes a habit. Before you know it, you've cut yourself off from one more aspect of life.

Life isn't a race in which the people with the most knowledge win. What's most important is to keep growing and learning. The real loss is when you hide from life altogether, afraid that your ignorance will become known.

Discounting What You Know Subliminally

Another way in which you may inhibit the change process is by discounting what you know subliminally or intuitively. I'm sure there are many things you know, but you don't actually know you know them until someone else says what you're thinking. As you learn to respect your subliminal knowledge, change will become easier for you, because you will be able to zero in on what the real problem is.

Gary said it well when he proclaimed, "There's a lot I learned in therapy that I already knew but had no access to. I knew it on a preconscious level. I wasn't clear or focused on it until my therapist brought it out into the open." Then he gave an example. "I'm usually uncomfortable when I'm with my brother-in-law, but I never knew why. My therapist said, 'He sounds like an intimidating person. When he says something, you fall silent. My guess is that you're feeling that you can't compete with him.' As soon as my therapist said that, I knew it was true." Once Gary understood the problem, he felt less vulnerable. Even if he didn't do anything differently, at least he knew what was going on and could, if he wished, develop a course of action to deal with it. As you begin to trust what you know beneath the surface, you'll find change easier.

Are You Ready?

The bravest thing you can do when you are not brave is to profess courage and act accordingly.

—Corra Harris

It's now time to roll up your sleeves and start learning the skills that will help you master your fears, triumph over your worries, and get on with your life.

"Nothing will ever be attempted," wrote Samuel Johnson, "if all possible objections must be first overcome." Just as this statement holds true for so many aspects of life, it's true for taming your fears. You probably have all sorts of reasons for why you can't change. You know your excuses. You're too busy. You're not sure if you'll succeed. You're hopeless. You're worried about the consequences. You're— afraid. Well, of course you are, but that's exactly why you need to make the commitment.

Once you take even the first few steps, the process of changing will seem much easier than it does when you stand at the start of the task without a blueprint for success. Take the leap of faith. Read on!

PART TWO

A Program for Change

5

Steps for Managing Your Mind

[People] *are not prisoners of fate, but only prisoners of their own minds.*

—Franklin D. Roosevelt

Have you ever taken a course on actively managing your mind? Have you ever read a book on learning how to think? I doubt it. Most people think they've learned how to think by attending school and learning information about the world. But schooling usually teaches you only one way of thinking: looking for the right answer. For this reason, you probably feel there's no need to think about thinking once you've got the right answer. There's no need to reflect on the ideas you have or the beliefs you maintain. There's no need to update your thinking skills.

But here's the problem with this approach. During adulthood, you have to deal with the ambiguities of life, challenges that don't have one right answer and problems that have no solutions. You need to figure out ways to strengthen and stretch your mind to deal with the constant change, the ups and downs, and the stresses and strains of life that don't have simple answers. If you don't, it's almost a given that you'll live your life in fear.

I find it interesting that in other areas of life, the importance of fitness is well accepted. I wouldn't be surprised if you have your own physical fitness regimen. Perhaps you exercise at home, or you've joined a gym, or else you work out with a personal trainer. I wouldn't be amazed, either, if you've taken the time to attend to your fiscal fitness by reading books on how to build a nest egg or by consulting with a financial planner. It's also likely to be true that you've learned a lot in recent years about the principles of weight management, time management, and money management.

But *mind* management? *Thought* management? I bet you haven't taken those into account.

I believe that if you haven't enhanced your thinking skills, you may very well be thinking in ways that are better geared to solving childhood problems than adult problems. Do you remember how you thought about the world when you were a kid? Like most youngsters, you probably thought about events, situations, and people in all-or-nothing terms. You were good or bad, did something right or wrong, and were in the "in" group or the "out" group. Fairy tales optimize this black-and-white thinking, too, with the good witch and the evil witch, the good fairy and the wicked stepmother, the guys in white hats and black hats. The "happily ever after" endings contribute to this simplistic type of thinking.

Most of us have learned the axiom, "It's not what you say, it's how you say it." Those words help us become more aware of our language and its effect on others. But have you ever heard the axiom "It's not what you think, it's how you think it?" Think about it! The way you think has a tremendous effect on you and how you react to the world. Your thought processes can either increase your fear or diminish it.

Small Decisions, Big Decisions

An essential part of mind management is having the ability to make good decisions without excessive anxiety. Modern life offers us more choices than ever before, which is a mixed blessing. Some choices are beneficial, while others just annoy us, confuse us, or make life more difficult.

Here's a personal example. I was in a small ski town in Vermont with my son Brian. We were going to catch a quick breakfast at Annie's Diner before heading out to the slopes. We both ordered orange juice, eggs (sunny side up), toast, and coffee. When we placed this simple order, we were met with a barrage of questions from a friendly waitress. Should the orange juice be small, medium, or large? Did we want fresh-squeezed or juice from concentrate? Should the eggs be well done or runny? And did we prefer toast: white, whole-wheat, raisin, rye, or pumpernickel? Then there was the issue of our coffee: did we want small, medium, large, or extra-large? Should it be regular or decaf? And did we prefer cream, half-and-half, whole milk, 2%, or nonfat milk?

Brian and I had the same reaction. All those choices for a simple breakfast! Helpful or bothersome? Our consensus was a bit of both. What amazed us was this: Isn't living in a small town supposed to be simpler than living in a big city? Aren't an abundance of choices supposed to be what you encounter at specialty shops like Starbucks, not at a country diner?

Modern life provides many other situations in which the multitude of options may easily overwhelm us. It could be a small matter, something you know isn't earth-shattering yet causes you to expend time and energy far out of proportion to the real issue. Perhaps you need to buy a suit. Should I buy this one or that one? Is it too expensive? Should I look elsewhere? Not being able to make up your mind can lead to making no decision at all, to being unhappy with the decision you do make, or to making rash decisions, such as overspending.

What about even more substantial decisions—whether to find a more challenging job, whether to get married, whether to get divorced, whether to have kids? I don't know if this is the right time. . . . I'm so afraid I can't handle the responsibility. . . . I'm terrified I'll make the wrong decision. . . . I'm forty years old—maybe it's too late! I should have taken this step earlier, made a different choice, made a better choice, planned it better, thought it through. . . . With all this indecisiveness comes panic and fear, and you still can't decide what you want to do.

How can you deal with the quandary of ambivalent thoughts? How can you discipline your mind to be more decisive? How can you think critically and creatively to make better choices? These questions are all crucial in a culture that provides us with a wealth of choices—perhaps more choices than we truly need. (In less affluent times, people just considered themselves lucky to acquire the bare necessities.) Good decision making and disciplined thinking aren't automatic, nor are they passive. Rather, they are skills that must be learned, updated, and revised as you chart your life course and meet new challenges.

This chapter will help you do just that.

Thinking or Obsessing?

One of the most important skills you can acquire as you tame your fears is learning to differentiate thinking from obsessing.

Andrea, who tends to be Hypervigilant, tries hard to sleep but has a tough time letting go of the day's worries. She can't stop obsessing about everything. About the laundry that needs to be done, the new car she wants to purchase, the birthday card she bought for her brother but forgot to send, the leak in the kitchen that needs attention, the huge loss in her stock portfolio that gives her an awful feeling in the pit of her stomach. "I can't stop thinking about these things," she says. "It drives me out of my mind. I can't relax, I can't sleep, and then, after tossing and turning all night, I'm so exhausted in the morning that it's hard to get up."

Andrea's repetitive, unproductive thought process isn't really thinking at all, it's obsessing, which doesn't solve the problems she's struggling with, and which increases and intensifies her fears. Obsessing is a vicious cycle she can't escape.

Here's how I'd explain the main difference between thinking and obsessing. Thinking includes reasoning, reflecting, pondering, regarding, judging, analyzing, or evaluating an idea. It is using your mind in a creative and effective manner. Thinking tends to be productive, goal-oriented, and action-oriented. Different forms of thinking include linear rational thinking, problem solving, brainstorming, and creative daydreaming.

An example of thinking is when you're sizing up your options for enrolling in an adult education course. You consider your choices, weigh the advantages and disadvantages of specific programs, imagine what certain courses would be like, and sort through the practical issues of transportation or financing your education.

By contrast, obsessing is when your mind is excessively occupied with a single emotion or idea that you can't let go of. Obsessing starts with Point A but doubles back on Point A over and over. It's true that obsessing is a form of thinking, but it's ineffective thinking; it goes around and around, spinning out of control, finally arriving at the exact same place where you began. This is not merely an unproductive process—it's counterproductive. Obsessing is always linked with anxiety, as the same thoughts are recycled without reaching any useful resolution. Fear and fatigue thrive in the closed circle of obsessing.

An example of obsessing would be this sequence of worries: "I really ought to take some college courses, but which ones? There are so many programs, I don't even know where to start! There's the local community college, but maybe that's not the right one for me. And there's the adult ed school, but those courses wouldn't lead to a degree. What should I study, anyway? Business courses? Health-related courses? Computer science? Something else? There are so many options that I don't know what to do. Maybe a technical institute is the way to go. But I'm not sure which field to consider. And how will I pay for my studies? Maybe with a loan. Or I could try for a grant. Or else—oh, I don't know *what* to do! But I really ought to take some sort of college course, shouldn't I? I feel so stuck."

The next two scenarios illustrate how to move from obsessing to thinking, ending with a satisfying plan of action.

Back to Work

Suppose you're struggling through a decision about whether to go back to full-time work now that your children are older. Obsessing over this kind of problem can quickly become an exhausting, fruitless exercise. "I really need to advance my career, but how will I ever manage?" you ask yourself. "What company would hire me, anyway? What if I don't get hired? I don't know how to update my résumé after all my years as a stay-at-home mom. I get so nervous. I won't be able to handle the interview."

Contrast this obsessive, circular process with thinking over the issue of going back to work. You tell yourself, "Well, let's see. This is a big decision to make, but maybe I can break it down into several steps, which will make it more manageable.

"Step One: I'll find someone to help me sort through the possibilities. I have friends and former coworkers who can help me speculate about my options. I'll make a few phone calls and see what they have to say. Step Two: I'll also update my résumé and write a sample cover letter. I can get that done by the end of next week. Step Three: The interview process can be unnerving, but I've done it before, so I guess I can do it again. Step Four: This plan sounds good, and I know it'll be beneficial to me in the long run. Now it's time to implement the decision. I'll talk with my friends first, then arrange for some informational interviews and maybe meet with a career counselor. I'll have to reorganize my schedule and delegate some of the domestic tasks, but I can do that, too. And even if life is hectic for a while, we'll all adjust."

As you can see, this thinking process doesn't make complex issues vanish, but it allows you to sort through them more systematically and deal with them one by one in a productive fashion.

Sweating the Market

Here's another scenario: obsessing about investments. "Oh my God!" you exclaim. "I've lost so much money in the market! How could I have been so stupid? Maybe I should sell now and cut my losses. Or should I buy now, since share prices are so low? But of course that's what I said last month and now look at how much more I lost this month! I'm just no good at this—I'll never make any money, and I may as well forget about retirement! And it was stupid of me to listen to my idiot brother-in-law!" Spinning in circles, you resort to hand-wringing, self-deprecation (you're a financial dope), character assassination (your brother-in-law is even worse), doom-and-gloom, and on and on, without any resolution about steps to take that will truly address the situation.

The alternative? Something much more even-tempered. You say, "Well, the market certainly has been a huge disappointment for the last few years. It's frustrating how much money I've lost since the boom went bust. But the question now is, What should I do about it? Here's a plan. Step One: I'm going to stay cool. Impulsive decisions will only make the situation worse. Step Two: I'll get more reliable advice. My brother-in-law may be well-intentioned, but he's not the financial wizard he imagines himself to be. I'm going to get some good, objective professional advice. Step Three: I'll work with that advisor to implement a better long-term strategy." Here again, thinking brings better results, requires less expenditure of physical and emotional energy, and has the added benefit of diminishing your fears.

How can you escape this nonstop mental misery? Here are two more steps you can take to change obsessing into more productive thinking. First, you have to get out of (or at least limit the time you spend in) the obsessing mode. To take this step, use the same techniques on yourself that you'd use on a two-year-old who's determined to play with the electric socket. Distract yourself with something else—something that absorbs your attention. Turn on the TV. Listen to music. Do a relatively easy task you've been avoiding, such as putting photos in an album. Call a friend. If you can use reading as a form of relaxation, try that, but make it easy reading because your obsessiveness may eat away at your attention and make it hard to concentrate.

Second, exercise can be an effective way to ease out of an obsessive state of mind. If you hate to exercise, simply *move*. Get off your butt and do something. It could be as simple as stretching your hands up to the sky, stretching your neck by looking behind you as far as you can, or taking a walk around the block. If you enjoy exercise, indulge yourself in a sport or other physical activity. It doesn't have to mean going off to the gym. You can go for a run. Play tennis. Do some yoga or t'ai chi. Practice deep breathing exercises. Movement and body work of many sorts are effective antidotes for obsessiveness. (In chapter 8 I'll offer detailed descriptions of these and other issues.)

If your mind is filled to the brim with one distressing thought after another, you've left precious little room for fresh, stimulating ideas. Once you've freed yourself from obsessing, you can begin to think in a more effective manner. The answer you may be looking for may already be knocking at your door but you won't be ready to hear it if you're preoccupied in other ways.

Now it's your turn to change your obsessing into practical, creative stepping-stones that will lead to good solutions.

Name three areas over which you have a tendency to obsess. They could involve a decision you need to make, an action you need to take, or a problem you need to solve.

1. _____

2. _____

3. _____

Now go back to what you've written and think about each one. On a piece of paper, write down three to five steps you're going to take to help you reach your decision, take your action, or solve your problem. Before you begin, I suggest that you take three deep breaths and in a gentle, reassuring voice, tell yourself, "I can do this." You've now set the stage for making a successful effort.

If you become stuck in this exercise, one of your steps can always be "I'll get more information about X," or "I'll discuss my dilemma with Y." (And make sure you choose someone whose intellect and empathy you trust.)

Avoid Paralysis of Analysis

Fear of trying causes paralysis.

—MASON COOLEY

Another type of futile thinking that emanates from fear is getting stuck in paralysis of analysis. Despite much researching, ruminating, and planning, you may find that you're not really making decisions or taking forward-going action. Paradoxically, the more analysis you do, the more you muddy the waters.

More May Not Be Better

Janice suffers from paralysis of analysis whenever she tries to make a decision about an important matter. As a Controlling person, she doesn't obsess about whatever situation she's facing; she just accumulates too much information. The result is that she gets bogged down in trying to make sense of it all. Recently, she has been attempting to decide where her four-year-old son, Kenneth, should go to kindergarten. "I like to be systematic about my options, " says Janice, "so I've gathered lots of data about the schools in our area. I don't want to miss any possibilities. Also, Kenneth is artistically gifted, and I want to make sure he'll attend a kindergarten that'll give him lots of interesting projects to challenge him." At first, Janice felt pleased to find more schools than she expected. But the sheer number and variety has grown confusing. "There are so many! I found some through the yellow pages, more through recommendations, and still more through a data search on the Web. Then I called these places and talked with the various directors on the phone. That's been great—I have a wealth of options to choose from. But the programs are so different! It's confusing to figure out how to compare one to another—or even whether some of these schools can be compared at all." To sort through the possibilities, Janice has created a chart listing the schools' attributes: size, cost, student-teacher ratios, special programs, and so forth. But it seems that the more data she compiles, the more confused she feels and—worst of all—the more fearful she feels that she'll somehow bungle the whole process and send Kenneth to a school that isn't really appropriate to his needs.

Enough Is Enough

Debbie prides herself on her competency and ability to manage the tasks in her life. During a recent project to renovate her family's bedrooms, however, she heard a startling accusation from her otherwise supportive thirteen-year-old daughter. "Jacqueline said, 'Ma, you're nuts. Just make a decision and stop driving everybody crazy over the bedrooms. I mean, these are only bedrooms!' And I realized she was right. I was absolutely *possessed* by the project. Every day was a new crisis. There was another decision to make, and I was so uncertain about what would be the best choice that I was driving everybody nuts—not only my family but the decorator and her assistants. I kept changing my mind every day and feeling dissatisfied with the choices I'd already made."

This realization led to some important insights. "I know my constant analyzing was making me lose my enthusiasm for the project," Debbie says. "I was agonizing over redoing the bedrooms and that was a shame, because I'd been looking forward to this project for years. That's when I recognized I had to calm down. Otherwise I'd ruin everything. It felt scary to actually let go and say, Okay, this is my choice—no more change. It was hard for me because I like to micromanage every little detail of a project. But I realize I don't know when to stop. I needed to remember that the decorator I'd chosen had an excellent reputation. So, why not trust her to actually get the job done? I didn't really need to second-guess her every move and analyze her every working moment."

My recommendation in a situation like this is to get smarter by thinking less about the issue that concerns you. It's possible that you've mistaken *more* thinking for *better* thinking. More thinking may only confuse the matter. Too many options, too much analysis, and too many choices can increase your paralysis. Don't feel you need every last bit of data to make a decision. Don't assume that extending the analysis of data on and on will necessarily produce a better outcome. All analyses reach a point of diminishing returns, and some good decisions take place relatively quickly, based as much on thoughtful intuition as on meticulous assessment of endless data.

EXERCISE: LIMBER UP AFTER PARALYSIS OF ANALYSIS

If paralysis of analysis is your nemesis, here are several ways to limber up and be more flexible.

1. Name a specific project that's taking up too much of your time. Now think about why you're having difficulty completing the task. I'll give you a head start by presenting you with a list of possibilities. Put a check mark next to every item that rings true for you.

    I'm spending too much time on this task (project/effort) because:

____ I want it to be perfect.

____ I procrastinate to avoid making a tough choice.

—— It makes me feel like an important, hard-working, busy person.

—— It gives me an excuse for not doing something else.

—— I'd rather not make any decision than make the wrong one.

—— I'm an idealist and hate settling for anything less than the best.

—— It fills up my free time, and I wouldn't know what else to do with that time.

—— I'm afraid what somebody else might say about my decision.

—— I have trouble with endings anyway.

—— When this project ends, I need to begin another one, and I'd rather not deal with that right now.

—— I'm an obsessive person—that's just the way I am.

—— I can never complete things until there's some crisis that makes me end it.

—— I paralyze myself by thinking What if.

—— I'm a better thinker than a doer; it's hard for me to leave the thinking stage.

Now come up with other reasons that I haven't covered. When you're finished, look back over your list and put a star next to the three top reasons for your paralysis of analysis.

2. Write a countering sentence to the reasons you've starred. Often this sentence can be the exact opposite of what you checked off. For instance, if you wrote, "I want it to be perfect," your countering sentence would be "I don't need it to be perfect." Or if you wrote, "It's a way I use to avoid making a tough choice," your countering sentence would be, "I can make this tough choice." At other times, you need to be more creative to obtain a countering sentence. For example, "It makes me feel like an important, hard-working, busy person" can be countered with "A hard-working, busy person isn't what I really want to be. I can enjoy life more if I stop making such a big project about everything I do."

Even if you don't believe your countering sentence right now, say it anyway. Say it out loud. Hear yourself say it. Let the countering statement sink in as a possibility. This exercise is an exploration. You aren't on the witness stand, where you have to tell the truth, the whole truth, and nothing but the truth. You are on an exploratory expedition, scouting out new ideas and investigating more effective ways of thinking.

3. To help you complete a project, create a time limit as well as a time budget for yourself.

    A time limit for Janice might be "I'll decide by next week which schools I'll select for Kenneth."

    The time budget for this effort might be as follows:

    - Searching the Internet for more information : 3 hours
    - Reviewing school brochures: 2 hours
    - Talking with a knowledgeable friend: 20 minutes
    - Assessing the information I have : 45 minutes
    - Discussing schools with spouse: 90 minutes
    - Filling out three applications to schools: 3 hours

    Now it's your turn to create a time limit and a time budget for your project. These times are not written in stone. They can be revised. Let them function as a guideline for you, designed to limit your paralysis of analysis and help you create closure.

Brainstorm in the Opposite Direction

"I hate my job," Marianne said. "I'd love to quit, but I'm afraid. I have a job that pays the bills and gives me health insurance, status, and respectability. I'm apprehensive about giving up those benefits, so I err on the side of caution."

"What if you didn't err on the side of caution?" I asked her. "What if you erred on the side of risk? Then what would you do?"

A smile immediately came to her face. Impishly she said, "I'd quit my job today, travel for a month, and start my own business the month after that."

Well, the way it worked out, Marianne didn't quit her job that day, but she did quit within six months. She erred on the side of risk—and that worked out well for her. She's now the owner of a small public relations firm. She loves her work, and she's heard from several people at her old PR firm who, as it turns out, were laid off.

"Who would know that when I took that gamble," Marianne told me recently, "it was not only the best thing I did for myself—it also turned out that I'm in a much less precarious position than my friends who stayed with the company."

But brainstorming isn't just a process of thinking in the opposite direction. It's also useful as a method for generating lots of possible solutions to a problem. You can do this by yourself, with a friend, or in a small group, such as your family. It's important not to reject a possible solution because it sounds ridiculous or seems as if it couldn't be done. With brainstorming, you allow your mind to take off in any direction in order to generate possible (not necessarily realistic or probable) solutions. If you can make an effort to counteract the way you habitually think, the outcome may surprise you. It's likely that you'll imagine possibilities that hadn't even occurred to you, possibilities that may take you in exciting new directions. Brainstorming enriches your thinking. It's easy to do. It won't hurt you to speculate about alternatives, and it doesn't cost a cent.

Brainstorming—a Group Effort

Here's an example of a small group and how its members use brainstorming. The Snyder family—Art, Jeri, and their two grown daughters, Lynnette and Lori—have a tradition of traveling together overseas during part of their summer vacation. They're anxious about travel, however, given the new reality of world events and threats toward Americans overseas. Art and Lynnette have discussed canceling this year's plans because of the risks. In response to this possibility, Jeri has urged her husband and daughters to brainstorm in order to find alternatives for a new family vacation. Each person can offer up any ideas that he or she finds interesting. The others will listen to those ideas as possibilities without initial criticism. Then the whole family will consider the options according to practicality, cost, and other criteria; they'll narrow the choices to a "short list" of three; they'll do research on them; and, finally, they'll take a vote.

The Snyders brainstormed these ideas:

- Jeri: "I say we try the Caribbean." Options: Jamaica, Bermuda, Aruba, or Puerto Rico.

- Art: "Let's stay fairly local." (The family lives in the Washington, D.C., area.) Options: the Outer Banks, the Blue Ridge, Colonial Williamsburg.

- Lynnette: "I'd like to see more of the western United States." Options: Colorado, Utah, Arizona, or California.

- Lori: "I just want to go to a place where there's swimming and snorkeling."

Obviously, the Snyder family has not yet reached a decision. They now need to narrow down the options so that they end up with a vacation that's satisfying to all. Brainstorming however, is a great start as it propels you beyond fearful, constricted thinking and on your way to more imaginative, resourceful ideas.

Reframe the Situation

Most people grow up thinking that what they assume to be true is, in fact, true. They don't realize that all of us construct a reality based on our experiences, our family histories, our biological sensitivities, our culture and religion, our predispositions, our learned biases, and our social network. We don't just live in the world—we actively interpret the world and our experiences in the world in a way that we consider natural. Anything outside of the way we think is then considered unnatural. This interpretation of our experiences is referred to as framing. Actively changing your interpretation is called reframing.

Construct a New Reality

Here's an example that I hope you can relate to. We all know people who look at the glass as half full and others who see it as half empty.

We call the first one an optimist and the second one a pessimist. Who is right? If you picked the optimist, congratulations! You chose the correct answer. If you picked the pessimist, congratulations to you too! You also chose the correct answer. Can there be two right answers? Absolutely, depending upon how you interpret your world.

If you want to change from being a pessimist to an optimist, or from a nervous person to a calm person, you need to learn how to reframe. In most situations, what's important is not the reality as such (there are four ounces of water in the glass) but rather how you *perceive* the reality. Do you interpret it as something bad or good? Do you look at what you have or what you don't have?

If you're living in fear, you have already developed a framework in which you habitually and automatically view many situations as scary—whether they are or not. It's time to break that habit of viewing situations through a foreboding lens and begin to look at the same situation in a different manner. Here's one way to do it.

You've been asked to teach a computer software program to supervisors in your company. The original frame: *scary!* Thoughts that go with this frame:

- I can't do this!
- How can I get out of this?
- I'm going to make a fool out of myself.
- Why me?

Rather than continue to interpret this situation as a problem, stop your thought process. Now reframe. Stretch your imagination and think: how else could I view this situation? Reframe: *exciting!* Thoughts that go with the reframe:

- What an opportunity!
- How can I make this work for me?
- This is a lucky break.
- This is a chance for me to shine.

When you reframe a situation, in addition to viewing your reality differently, you may need to do something differently to make your new interpretation successful. In the previous example, changing your frame from scary to exciting is the first part of the process. The second part is working hard to make sure that, indeed, you do shine. If you neglect to take the action to back up your new thinking, it may well backfire on you, leaving you further entrenched in your original interpretation. ("You see, it *is* scary. I *did* do a terrible job.") At other times, reframing doesn't need any backup action. It's simply enjoying an innovative way of thinking.

Do you want to learn creative ways to reframe a situation? Listen to young children who haven't yet been brainwashed to think that everything has a right answer—and that the right answer is what somebody else thinks it is.

Here are two of my favorite examples.

Kids are Great Reframers

When my son Daniel was still a preschooler, he taught me a lesson about reframing that I'll never forget. Danny was a determined, self-assured little boy. One afternoon, when I'd had enough of his misbe-having, I decided to take action. Short-tempered myself, I pulled Danny down the hallway and shoved him into his room. As I slammed the door behind him, I hissed, "Now you stay there!" Without missing a beat, Danny reopened the door, slammed it in my face, and yelled, "You can't come in!"

As I walked away from his room, I chuckled at this kid's moxie. I could make him stay in his room, but I couldn't take away his personal power. He had reframed the situation to make it a punishment for *me*. Coming from a background in which I often felt intimidated by others, I was very impressed that Danny could reframe a situation at the age of three. I thought to myself, "If *he* can do it, *I* can do it." Since then, remembering this event has been my confidence-booster in many a difficult moment. What a joy when you raise your child to think for himself and then he becomes a role model for you!

Here's another story about a kid who reframed her situation, but the parent didn't know enough to be impressed by her ability.

Walter was irritable the day he picked up his six-year-old daughter, Amelia, from soccer practice. Looking in the rearview mirror, he saw Amelia without her seat belt on. Walter barked, "Stop jumping around! Get that belt on right now and sit still!"

Amelia obeyed. A few minutes later, he noticed her sitting with her arms folded and an impish smile on her face. Walter asked her what was so funny. Amelia responded, "You can make me sit still, but I'm still jumping around on the inside."

Too bad Walter knew nothing about the concept of reframing. He couldn't acknowledge the creativity and intelligence in his daughter's response. He never got beyond his interpretation that she was disrespectful. So when they arrived home, Walter punished Amelia for the transgression of "jumping around on the inside."

Free Yourself from the Outcome

Until a generation ago, most people assumed that they couldn't control the outcome of many of life's events. People accepted that events simply occurred; you didn't make them happen. Children "arrived," they weren't planned. You didn't agonize over the ideal career, you just "fell into a job." Nowadays, however, because we really do have more control over our lives, we feel anguished when we can't control our fate.

If you can free yourself from expecting that the outcome must always be in your favor, your fears will diminish. This doesn't mean that you should become indifferent to what happens as a result of your choices and actions. Rather, it means that you need to accept this reality: Although you can make decisions and act in response to situations, you can't *force* specific events to happen. You can't always be in control.

Do What You Gotta Do

Roy, a forty-two-year-old divorced Shy man, is well aware that he fears rejection. He's been wanting to ask Serena out on a date for some time. But as soon as he begins to think about doing this, he focuses on what might go wrong. "I start off feeling excited about asking her out, but then my fears take over. What if she rejects me? What if she thinks I'm not good enough for her? What if she already has a boyfriend? After all this agonizing, I do nothing."

Roy's chronic uneasiness with asking Serena out occurs because he has tied his success to Serena's response. Freeing himself from the outcome means that it doesn't matter what his would-be date does or doesn't do. What matters is that he takes the action that's within his ability to control: asking Serena out on a date.

A Different Kind of Courage

Here's a more complex, more emotionally wrenching example of this same issue. Ethan grew up in a family of strong men—"men of courage," as he calls them. His father, two of his uncles, and his brother were all firefighters. In Ethan's family, fearful experiences were routine matters, hence not very frightening. But then again, nothing tragic had ever occurred, and harrowing experiences made for good storytelling. Competitive athletics were also a major part of life. Mottoes such as "no pain, no gain" and "second place is loser's place" were indelibly etched in Ethan's brain from childhood on.

Given his background and macho orientation, courage seemed synonymous with masculinity. If you weren't courageous—if you couldn't face the music, take the heat, keep your chin up, toe the line—you risked being thought of as a coward. Ethan's family defined courage in terms of physical strength, firmness of mind, and "just doing it."

But now Ethan was facing a completely different kind of challenge. His wife, Janine, forty-three years old, had just been diagnosed with pancreatic cancer. His initial reaction was predictable: "We're going to fight this," "We'll beat the odds," "We won't let it get the best of us."

But as time passed, as chemotherapy treatments went on, and as the disease progressed, Janine became more and more upset with Ethan's frame of mind. Finally she spoke up, beginning with those words that men dread hearing: "We need to talk."

"About what?" he responded.

"Ethan, I need you to accept that I'll probably die. When you keep telling me to fight and fight and fight, I feel worse, not better. You make me feel like I'm a failure. Of *course* I want to live, but I know that's doubtful." Ethan found these words baffling and difficult to hear. Janine pressed the point: "I need you to be there with me—not with bravado but with acceptance. Otherwise, I can't speak freely to you. I can't tell you how sorry I am that I'll be leaving you and how afraid I am for Daria. Please don't forget she's only twelve years old. She has to be able to talk with someone about what's happening. I don't want you to make her feel that she has to be strong when she's not feeling strong at all. I don't want that for her—for you or for me."

For the first time in his life, Ethan needed a different kind of courage. He needed to do something far different from fighting every inch of the way. He needed to free himself from the outcome. He could hope that Janine would beat the disease, but he couldn't *make* that happen—no matter how hard he tried. And neither could she. "Giving a hundred and ten percent" was no longer relevant, as it was in sports. "Not shrinking from your duty" had no meaning. This was a new kind of challenge for Ethan.

This kind of courage meant accepting whatever happened and relinquishing control. Ethan needed simply to be with his wife, not to fight the enemy. The crisis that Ethan faced was a force out of his control, one that he had never dealt with before. His challenge was to accept the situation and listen to the people he loved. His task was simply to be there, not to do.

This was a new kind of courage, a test for which he was totally unprepared: letting go as courage.

Plan and Let Go

Perfectionists, in particular, create a lot of fear for themselves because their only definition of success is everything working out just right. But life doesn't often present situations in which everything works out just right. Consider the stock market. If you lost "only" 10 percent of your retirement fund during a year in which the S&P lost 25 percent, you might feel delighted with your approach to investing. A perfectionist like Jim, however, would be horrified that he'd lost anything at all. Not only would he lament the loss of money, he'd also perceive the situation as justifying his fear that "he can't do anything right." As he moans and groans about his loss, he intensifies the emotional effects.

Freeing yourself from the outcome in this situation means that you have a financial plan you feel satisfied with, but you also accept that even sound financial planning doesn't guarantee returns on your money every year. It also means that if you take a loss, it doesn't imply that you (or the person who handles your finances) did anything wrong. You simply suffered the temporary consequences of the market's normal ups and downs. Similarly, freeing yourself from the outcome doesn't guarantee success in getting a date, landing a plum job, or getting your children to behave well. None of those outcomes is fully in your control. It's worthwhile to work hard, communicate well, and keep your eyes on the prize, but constant worry—and a fixation on one particular outcome—won't really help you attain your goals. Instead, I recommend that you focus your mind on what you've decided is the best course of action for you at this particular time. Do what you can, then let go.

Exercise: Free Yourself from the Outcome

Here are some examples of how you can reframe situations so that you free yourself from the outcome:

- Instead of thinking: I've got to get this job.

  Think: I'll do a thorough preparation for the interview and whatever happens, happens.

- Instead of thinking: I'm afraid to ask him to lend me money.

  Think: I'll ask and explain why I'm asking. If he says no, I'll think of plan B.

- Instead of thinking: I'm afraid of what the doctor will say about this lump I feel.

  Think: I can't control what's happening in my body, but I can take a supportive friend with me to the doctor so that I don't have to be alone, just in case it's bad news.

Now, let's consider your personal situation.

1. Name a situation in which you need to let go of the outcome.

_____

2. Now reframe your thinking from being result-oriented to action-oriented.

- Instead of thinking: _____
- I need to think: _____

Try this shift of attitude on another personal situation:

- Instead of thinking: _____
- I need to think: _____

Cultivate a Relaxed Mind

It's easy to say, "Just relax," but for many people, that's a really tough thing to do. However, it's still a great goal to pursue. If you can attain a relaxed state of mind, you're less likely to fall into repetitive, obsessive thought patterns. You'll think more clearly and experience less fatigue as you deal more thoughtfully with choices and decisions.

Looking for Danger

Joan, a thirty-four-year-old mother of two, is definitely a Hypervigilant type. She's the kind of person who focuses on danger wherever she goes. Whenever she looks for danger, she finds it. She's inclined to make tough moments bigger, more threatening, or more awful than they really are. She recently admitted to ruining a family ski trip because of her worries that either she or someone else in the family would break a leg.

Joan needed to learn how to cultivate a relaxed mind. With a mind that's tight and tense, it's hard to unwind or enjoy yourself. How can you relax your gray matter? One way is to shift the focus from what's threatening to what's exciting or promising about a situation. Joan couldn't help it if a fearful thought popped into her mind, but she could and did learn to develop control over how long that thought stayed there. She developed this skill by reminding herself why she had planned the ski trip in the first place — it was supposed to be fun, a great family vacation, and a chance to be outdoors together.

Not only does being Hypervigilant spoil all the fun, it also drains your energy without increasing your safety. Although unexpected events and setbacks are part of life, staying on constant alert for catastrophe isn't helpful; on the contrary, it can be exhausting and counterproductive. Even when an event is truly horrific, it's healing to reassure yourself with calming, not alarming, messages following the initial shock and acute stress. "I'll get through it," you can tell yourself. "I can reach out for support during this difficult time," or "I don't know when, I don't know how, but I will find a way to cope with this."

Lightening a Burden

"When I was a kid," Rick says, "life was easier than it is now. I went to school, played ball, rode my bike, watched TV. I had no major problems. But now I feel much more vulnerable. I have a perfectionist wife and two sons who need to be dealt with, supervised, driven places. I have a lot of pressure on me to make a good living so that they can do all the activities they're involved in. If I don't measure up, I feel like I'm failing them."

Rick finds that his wife's expectations put him under a lot of pressure. "I want to please my wife, but it's getting harder for me to do that. When we first met, she liked that I was easygoing. Now, she can't stand it. She's merciless in her judgments about what I've done and haven't done. Instead of my influencing her to relax a bit, she's been influencing me to become more tense. I know I don't want things to continue this way."

Faced with this tense marriage, Rick has struggled to find ways to vent his frustrations and diminish his stress level. "To make myself more relaxed," he explains, "I've installed basketball nerf sets in my offices at home and at work." Shooting baskets is just a small but effective release valve for Rick's tensions. "I've also been listening to music from my teen years, and I get together with some musician buddies once a week to jam. These things may seem insignificant, but I actually find they help me to feel more like my old relaxed teenage self." More important, Rick and his wife have started marriage counseling, which is giving them a place to air their grievances and misunderstandings. They're now learning to respect each others' differences and talk things out before they become more damaging.

Tips on Cultivating a Relaxed Mind

- Listen to music. Any kind that soothes your soul will fit the bill.

- Take a warm bath. Few things can relax you faster than a long soak. Indulge yourself in bubbles, if you like.

- Sit by the fireplace. Do nothing but stare for twenty minutes. Let yourself be hypnotized by the flames.

- Buy a Zen water fountain. Listen to the whisper of water in motion.

- Use humor. Tell a joke. Listen to a joke. Enjoy what's goofy or silly in life.

- Use your imagination. Create a place in your mind where you can go to feel safe, warm, cozy, and comfy. Imagine staying there for as long as you need to, until your mind is quiet and your body is relaxed. Don't emerge until you're ready.

A relaxed body is a good home for a relaxed mind. In chapters 9 and 10, I'll provide suggestions for how to relax the body.

6

Steps for Altering Your Attitudes

The policy of being too cautious is the greatest risk of all.

—JAWAHARLAL NEHRU

"THE GREATEST DISCOVERY," wrote William James, "is that a human being can alter his life by altering his attitudes of mind." Life presents us with many challenges, some of which rightly prompt a sense of danger. But by using your mind to size up your situation, calculate your best course of action, and stay resolute, you can master your fears.

Limit Your Exposure to the Media

It's not an easy job to keep your fears in check—particularly in this era of mass media. As if our individual fears aren't sufficiently intense, we can count on the mass media to throw gasoline on the fire. Newspaper headlines, magazine articles, TV programs, and Web sites trumpet the appalling dangers we all face.

Here are just a few recent examples of fear-oriented articles in the media:

- A *Time* magazine cover story ("The Columbine Effect") describes a new fear of parents and children: "kids pulling a Columbine."

- Another *Time* magazine cover story ("What Scares You?") reports that 50 million Americans suffer from debilitating fears.

- Even *Glamour* magazine, whose mission is fashion and style, gave prominence on a cover to two fear inducing stories: "'I Thought It Was Cancer'—Every Lump and Bump Explained" and "21 Rape Preventions the Police Urge You to Read: Lifesaving Do's and Don'ts."

The mass media exaggerates dangers to create a more sensational story. For example, news reports go into great detail about the risks of terror attacks. While this issue certainly merits concern, most Americans are at greater risk from more routine, less exotic dangers, such as food poisoning or car accidents. The reality of the market-place, however, is that scary headlines sell newspapers and increase the viewing of TV programs.

Right after the September 11 attacks, when everyone in the United States was still gripped with fear, we all heard messages that made it difficult to know how we should live our lives. The authorities told us to watch for suspicious mail, keep alert, be wary of unusual activity, and keep our antennae up for suspicious-looking people. But they also nagged us to please return to normal. Huh? As Philip Zimbardo, former president of the American Psychological Association, states, "It's impossible to maintain a state of constant personal alertness. Something has to give." Sooner or later the human mind needs relief from the tension between advice to stay alert and advice to relax. During the immediate post-September 11 period, how were we sup-posed to reconcile the two separate, contradictory sets of advice? How were we supposed to be constantly vigilant yet able to proceed normally, as if nothing unusual was going to happen?

These were important questions not only for the days following September 11 but also for right now. How can we go about our every-day business and not be frightened when every newspaper, TV screen, and Internet news site proclaim the horrific new dangers? Summer brings shark attacks! Winter brings deadly storms! Childhood brings accidents, illnesses, abduction! Midlife brings set-backs, strain, challenges! Old age brings hardships, losses, disability! And we always hear horror stories of airplane crashes, train wrecks, fatal car accidents, child abuse, and now terrorist threats and attacks, international tensions in Iraq, and the hazards of nuclear weapons in North Korea. My advice is to limit your exposure to media madness. Downplay the media's hysteria. Correct for the media's tendency to overdramatize the presentation of news information.

One way to reduce our fear is to *assess* risk rather than seek to *avoid* risk. Wearing a seat belt downgrades your risk of dying or being seriously injured in a car accident. Does this precaution eliminate all the dangers of traveling in a car? Of course not. Is this step worth taking? Very much so. Ironically, though, many people focus on dangers that are relatively safe and are haunted by those that are less likely to happen. They'll obsess about the hazards of air travel yet drive without using a seat belt. They'll be alarmed about radiation risks from a nuclear plant yet be blasé about radiation risks from the sun. I suggest you live your life in a relatively safe way, but without sacrificing your quality of life.

Risk Analysis

People vary in the amount of risk they find comfortable. We all need to contemplate our acceptable risk-reward ratio. Sara wondered whether to go to her lunch date on a day when the National Weather Service issued a severe weather advisory for her area. She decided not to go, since the risk (a bad day for driving) was so disproportionate to the payoff (an outing that could easily be rescheduled). On the same day, Georgette decided to attend her brother's wedding; the reward far outweighed the risk she faced.

What risks are you willing to take to live your life? When are you being overly cautious? When are you taking excessive risks? There are no right or wrong answers to these questions. Each of us needs to reach our own conclusions. However, risk is less frightening when we understand it better. Here are a few things to keep in mind:

- *An activity's inherent risk isn't the same as how risky we perceive it to be.* For instance, most people feel that flying is riskier than driving, even though they've been told repeatedly that we're statistically more likely to die in a car than in a plane. Logic often has little influence over our emotional reactions.

- *When we are in control (for instance, as the driver of a car), we tend to feel less vulnerable than when someone else is in control.* As a passenger in a plane, we must put our trust and faith in strangers. Those who have difficulty relinquishing control will usually experience more fear in those types of situations. Backseat driving is so prevalent precisely because many folks can't relax when someone else is in control—even someone they know well.

- *New risk is scarier than old risk.* You're much more likely to die of the flu than of an anthrax infection. But since the flu is a "known" disease and anthrax is "new" (or at least new in public awareness), anthrax seems more lethal and much scarier.

- *Newspaper and TV images of dreadful events make them more vivid in our imagination.* Plane crashes, hurricanes, and other high-profile disasters create intense anguish. Overexposure to such events make us believe that they happen more frequently than they really do.

There's no absolute safety in this world. Indeed, even staying home is a fairly risky business, since home is where many fatal accidents occur. As a result, it's crucial to distinguish between how risky a situation actually is and how risky it feels. Be guided not only by the fear in your gut but also by the knowledge in your head.

Delight in Difficulty

If you have a tendency to regard *difficult* as automatically synonymous with *arduous, demanding, onerous, exhausting, troublesome, tedious, impossible, unmanageable,* and *unacceptable,* you'll tend to feel more anxious whenever you think about doing a difficult task. Yet difficulty doesn't need to be burdensome or negative. You can also think of it as challenging, expanding your comfort zone, or inviting you to build new skills that you never thought you could acquire. Difficulty isn't just something to tolerate, endure, and suffer through; it can also be a source of pride, delight, or self-fulfillment.

When my cousin Carole passed away, her husband, George, asked me if I would give the eulogy at her funeral service. His request came as a surprise to me. Not because I wasn't close to Carole—I definitely was—but because I'd just never imagined doing something like that. My first impulse was to decline as gently as possible. The eulogy would be too difficult; I'd be too emotional.

It took me a few hours to get past my anxiety, but when I did, I realized that my answer could be nothing but Yes. I loved Carole dearly. It was an honor to be asked to speak at her funeral. I just had to get past the stage of "I can't do this" to "How am I going to do this?" Once I was able to relax a bit, I knew just how I wanted to begin. With tears in my eyes, I started to write: "They say you can pick your friends but not your family. But with Carole, I had the best of both worlds. I had family and friend, all wrapped up in the same person."

When the eulogy was completed, I was so glad I'd done it. I would have regretted it immensely if I hadn't. I felt proud of what I contributed to my cousin's honor on this solemn occasion.

It's a Jungle Out There

Here's another example of my "delight-in-difficulty" philosophy. In 1996, my globe-trotting son Glenn asked me if I'd visit him if he accepted a new job in Uganda. "Boy, you're really testing my mettle this time," I quipped. "Russia was one thing. The Ukraine was another. But Idi Amin's old stomping ground? I don't think so." The trip would be too difficult, too far away, too scary. My husband had just started a new job, so I'd have to travel by myself. But I had promised Glenn that wherever he was, I'd visit him, and I take pride in keeping my promises. So I had to make good on my motto to delight in difficulty.

Although my heart was beating fast as I boarded my flight to Uganda, I was more astonished than afraid that I was actually taking the trip. What an unlikely event that I—someone not known for bravery—should be flying solo to a country I'd never have imagined visiting. But that was only the start of my discovery of how quickly my world was expanding—and how exciting it would become.

A few days later Glenn and I left the relative comfort of Kampala, Uganda's capital, and started on our sojourn to the Bwindi Impenetrable Forest in search of mountain gorillas. Almost extinct, these animals now live in protected rain forests. Only a few adventurous souls are allowed to climb the mountains with a guide to visit with these gentle giants.

The mountains stretched ahead of us for miles. The roads were primitive, the curves steep, the night pitch black. I felt petrified when armed guards stopped our vehicle. With my heart pounding, I couldn't help but imagine the headlines: "Long Island Woman and Son Shot in Remote Mountains of East Africa." I couldn't help but question my sanity. What the hell am I doing here? Who am I kidding? This is a terrible mistake—I want to go home!

"Have a nice trip," the soldiers told us with a smile.

"Mom, those were the *good* guys," Glenn told me as he noticed my terrified expression.

"Oh, great!" I said as we continued on our way.

As we continued to climb the treacherous mountain road, my imagination had revised the headline only slightly: "Long Island Woman and Son Die in Plunge Off Mountain Road."

Okay, so I'm still afraid, I told myself. But look where I am. Maybe it's better to be scared *during* an adventure than to be scared about adventures that never take place.

We arrived late that night at our campground. Early the next morning, we trekked on foot through the mountains "following the dung," as the guides put it, until we located a family of gorillas. To protect the gorillas from us, we were allowed to be no closer than five feet from them, and we had to sit quietly (cameras operating, of course) to observe them in the wild. The silverback (all 600 pounds of him) was too busy resting and sleeping to pay us much attention— thank goodness for small favors! But the gorilla kids, five of them in all, were as fascinated with us as we were with them. And the mother's gaze was intense as she protectively watched her children reach out to us. (As a psychologist, I couldn't help wondering if this was the original model of a "functional family.")

"You were a trouper, Mom," Glenn told me two days later. "And weren't those gorillas worth it?"

They were. They truly were.

Was the trip difficult? I'd never claim it wasn't. Was it delightful? You bet—and all the more so for being difficult.

Ways to Feel Delight in Difficulty

You may not view yourself as a person who thinks that doing difficult things is delightful. Indeed, you may think that your m.o. is just the opposite. Shying away from the tough stuff, you excuse yourself by saying "I can't" or "I'm uncomfortable with that." Well, think again. I bet you have your own story about tackling a task that was troublesome, and I'm sure you feel proud that you succeeded despite your fears. Let me stir your memory by giving you some examples.

- *You rose to a challenge.* Eighty-three-year-old Alice thought she could never learn to use a computer. Now she e-mails her grandchildren and great-grandchildren on a regular basis.

- *You decided to do it because it was important to you.* John, confined to a wheelchair, traveled 3,000 miles to his brother's wedding despite the many hardships he had to endure.

- *You chose to do it because it might be fun, even though it was hard work.* Dan, generally a laid-back, let-it-be person, psyched himself up to train for the New York City marathon and completed it in excellent time.

- *You did it just to see if you could.* Gail never imagined her thoughts were important, yet she challenged herself to see if she could get her letter published in her local paper. Sure enough, she did.

- *You took an action because you're sick and tired of being an ostrich, with your head in the sand.* Alex felt terrified of going for an AIDS test but decided, "Enough avoidance—I need to stop fooling myself."

- *You knew that you've always done difficult things, but* delight *in them?* June never shied away from responsibility or hard tasks, but she never delighted in them. She was raised to regard tooting her own horn as a sin. Hence, it was unique for June to celebrate with friends her eighty-pound weight loss.

Appreciate How Time Makes Many Things Easier

We often don't appreciate how time will enhance our ability to deal with what we need to face. Because we're too frightened to do something now, we act as though that fear will always be present with the same intensity. Let's say that you were terrified of going to sleep-away camp as a nine-year-old, and you had a tough time adjusting during that summer so long ago. As a young adult, you may have faced other separations from the people you love, such as going off to college. Now you have to travel on business trips, which are difficult in their own way. Is it always a snap? Probably not. Do you still feel anxious about going away? Perhaps you do. But I bet your anxiety isn't nearly as strong as it was when you were nine years old. Keep in mind that many difficult or anxiety-producing tasks *do* get easier over time. If you can be patient with yourself and give yourself some leeway, you'll master tasks you never thought you could, and add coping with them to your tool kit of life skills.

As in the story of the ugly duckling—or in the case of an awkward teen—giving time a chance usually works in our favor. We can let our beauty, our talent, and our abilities evolve—if only we don't give ourselves such a hard time just because we can't do something right now.

Two examples follow.

On-the-Job Training

Drew, currently in medical school, feels overwhelmed by the demands on his time, energy, and stamina. "How am I ever going to know enough to be a competent doctor?" he asks, anguished about the massive amounts of information he must internalize. "I'll have people's lives in my hands. I don't know if I chose the wrong profession. Maybe I can't hack it." It's easy to understand why Drew's thinking is marred by self-doubts—medical school is notoriously stressful—but he needs to trust that in the long run he'll be able to learn what he needs to know. Medical school takes a long time for good reason. All those years of study (plus internship and residency) create knowledge, skills, and confidence that aren't possible to acquire quickly. Drew has to trust that what seems impossible now will become familiar and routine in later years.

Of course, not many people go through medical school. But the same situation I'm describing holds true for a highly demanding but far more common experience: parenthood. When you first become a parent, it's hard to imagine how you'll ever know everything necessary to raise a child. If you worry about all the many upcoming stages of parenthood and the multitude of skills you must acquire, you'll quickly sink into fear, even dread. "I'm having twins," Sandra says, expressing a mix of delight and alarm. "Jack and I are thrilled, but I have to tell you—I'm really scared. I just don't know how I'm going to handle it. I can barely imagine coping with *one* kid, so how in the world am I going to handle *two*?" Sandra's apprehension is common among new parents. To ease her worries, she needs to recognize that she doesn't have to know everything about parenthood the day after her sonogram. Raising children is the ultimate on-the-job training. Sandra will learn what she needs to learn over time. She'll develop the skills she needs by practice, by networking, by reading books, and by taking courses. She needs to give herself the time to learn the ropes as a parent.

Making a Molehill out of a Mountain

Time helps us get used to new realities, such as color-coded terror alerts, luggage searches, and divorce. Time also changes our perspective in many ways: Issues we used to think were major, we can learn to view as the small stuff. Doreen made one of these shifts by operating in accordance with what she calls her five-year principle. "I ask myself, 'Will this matter in five years?'" Doreen says. "If not, what am I worrying about? It's amazing how using this rule makes so many problems go away."

Even when something *is* a big deal, however, time can help us adjust. Gina even got accustomed to chemotherapy. Before her first treatment, she was terrified about what would happen. Her fear diminished greatly by her fifth treatment. Indeed, she thought of it more as an annoyance but not a fear, for she now knew what to expect both during the treatment and afterward.

Many people mellow as time goes on. Age, experience, and trust all contribute to this shift in attitude. We learn that many things we regard as important just aren't so earth-shattering after all, and many things we fear never end up happening.

With the passage of time:

- Alex, who's a Shy person, now feels less self-conscious about talking in front of a group.

- Jerry, a Macho type, sandpapered his rough edges. Once a tough dad, he shocked his grown children (and made them rather jealous) when he became a tender and caring grandfather.

- Compliant Beverly became more sure of herself, more seasoned, more assertive, and more outspoken.

- Controlling Phil became less compelled to orchestrate and fix other people's problems when he realized how much he was alienating the people he loved.

- Hypervigilant Barbara became more trusting that danger wasn't lurking around every corner. She could relax once she acknowledged that others (particularly her children) had good heads on their shoulders and could watch out for themselves.

Now what about you? Can you name something in your life that became easier over time? If so, let this memory soothe you in the middle of the night when you're having trouble falling asleep. Let it comfort you in the middle of the day when you get a sinking feeling in the pit of your stomach. Keep reminding yourself that most concerns work out well, and most burdens get easier over time.

Develop Resilience and Hardiness

You may consider yourself anything but hardy, robust, and resilient. Indeed, you may think of yourself as fear-prone, overly sensitive, timid, delicate, frail, rigid, tense, inflexible, unable to adapt well, easily alarmed by the future, and intent on having things a certain way. This may sound like a lot of wearisome attributes, but let's face it, fear-prone people don't find life a breeze. But the way we begin life doesn't need to be the way we continue to live. People do change, becoming more resilient and hardy as time goes on.

There are people (Theodore Roosevelt comes to mind) who were sickly, fragile children yet grew up to be strong in spirit as well as in body. Such people focus on what they *can* do, not what they can't. So instead of continuing to fixate on your weaknesses, wouldn't it be great to remind yourself that you, too, have strengths? That you've tolerated life's ups and downs, and that doing so has made you more resilient than before? Even if you don't adapt easily to change, wouldn't it be gracious of you to give yourself at least some credit for having gotten through some rough times? Maybe you can recognize that you're a better person for it. Instead of continuing to think of yourself as timid or weak, surely there have been moments when you've been strong and determined. Hey, you've done it! Why not acknowledge it?

The truth is, most people are tougher than they give themselves credit for being. You can—and you will—survive hard times. Not only that, but most of the time you'll emerge from the experience stronger and wiser.

Figure and Background

Ann is an example of how a woman who felt weak and powerless developed a much stronger sense of self over time. "I've always been aware of my limitations but unaware of my possibilities," Ann confessed. "Growing up felt different from other kids because my mother and father were Holocaust survivors. My parents wouldn't talk about what they went through, but I knew it was horrendous. They were the only members of their families to survive. If I had experienced the Holocaust myself, I doubt that I would have been strong enough to survive it."

On emigrating to this country, Ann's father became a hard-working, successful businessman. Yet, as Ann explains, "There was always a dark feeling in our household. My parents came from nothing and ended up wealthy, but none of that success brought joy to our family." Her parents' trauma created a complex legacy for Ann. "I grew up feeling that I was weak. And I was ashamed of my weakness," she states. "My parents had to be strong to live through the Holocaust. What would they think of me if I couldn't handle my own problems—which were so insignificant compared to what they had to endure? Growing up, I had feelings I didn't know how to deal with. I never felt good enough. I never felt smart enough. All of my problems felt trivial. How could I complain about a low grade when my mother could never smile? How could I say what frustrated me when my father was so steeped in pain? Though they survived, they did not survive with their spirit intact."

When Ann joined a support group for children of Holocaust survivors, she discovered that she wasn't alone in experiencing this psychic unrest. As an only child, she had never before had anyone to share her feelings with about her unusual family background. The group helped her recognize how her family's history affected her perceptions of the world and of herself. One insight, in particular, was most meaningful: how she polarized her world, feeling weak, powerless, and ineffective at home, but feeling strong, powerful, and competent away from home.

At college she took an introductory psychology course. One lesson that especially intrigued her was perceptual experiments that illustrated the concepts of figure and background. She found one particularly fascinating: a drawing that, depending on how you looked at it, could be seen in two ways—either as an old woman or as a fashionable young woman. First, you could make out only one figure or the other. But once you saw both of them, your mind could switch back and forth between the two. This ability to switch was a "Eureka!" experience for Ann. She recognized that she too could switch back and forth between being a weak, helpless girl and a strong, sturdy woman.

In response to these insights, Ann knew that even if her weak, helpless girl part was temporarily the "figure," the strong, sturdy woman was always hanging around in the background, and could emerge at any time. To help that stronger self surface, she has cultivated reassuring thoughts, such as telling herself, "Yes, I can do that," instead of defeatist thoughts, such as "It's too much for me." And she reminds herself that even if she does mess up, it won't be the end of the world. She won't fall apart, ruin everything, or have a nervous breakdown.

On the Outside Looking In

There's another issue I'd like you to consider. You may think of yourself as not very strong or resilient partly because you compare yourself with other people. In doing so, you take into account only what you see on those folks' outside, not on the inside. You are unaware of the struggles that even confident, competent people have endured. You may imagine that you're the only person fighting an uphill battle with the particular issues you face, but that's rarely, if ever, true.

This outlook can lead to a belief that others have no troubles; they don't grapple with choices or decisions; they're blessed because everything goes well for them; there are no seams, faults, or stress lines in their lives. Like a perfect wedding, those people's lives look so beautiful, so flawless. Well, perhaps a few people in this world may have such an easy time, but the vast majority of us are somewhere in the middle. Our lives are basically good but fraught with challenges, difficulties, and daily problems. And even the people who seem to skate through life may have more struggles than you can imagine. The week before the picture-perfect wedding, you didn't have an opportunity to see the bride in tears when her dress didn't fit right, and you didn't hear her parents screaming at each other because someone hadn't taken care of this or that.

One of the reasons I love to read biographies—especially about people during their early years—is to learn how people have overcome their own personal obstacles. Although the subjects of those books may not be our contemporaries or in our social class, they reveal how even famous people have needed to surmount severe doubts and fears to achieve greatness. You, too, can prevail over tough times. You, too, are capable of bouncing back after a mistake or a tragedy. And you, too, can recover your inner confidence as you let go of the regrets, the grudges, the grievances, the rigidity that binds you to your past. Believe in yourself and you'll be surprised and pleased at how resilient you can be.

Pay Attention to Your Senses

The way some people live, you'd think that nothing in this world matters except their mind. But as important as your mind can be, it can run away with you, creating catastrophes, crises, and emergencies when there's actually just a detour or a bump in the road—or perhaps no problem at all.

One way to change your overemphasis on thinking is to pay more attention to your senses. Stretch, take a deep breath, and let go of any chores you must do or problems you must solve. Then do the following exercise:

1. Take an apple out of the refrigerator. (Some other fruit or vegetable will serve the purpose just as well.)

2. Set it on the table.

3. Sit and make yourself comfortable.

4. Now look at the apple in front of you as though it's the first apple you've ever seen. Never mind that you've seen a thousand apples before—stare at it as if it's a strange, exotic object, something from another continent, another world.

5. Take careful note of what you see.

6. Touch it, noticing the texture, and be aware of how it feels in your hand, whether it's smooth or rough.

7. Describe the feeling to yourself.

8. Now close your eyes and bite into the apple.

9. Pay close attention to the taste in your mouth and the smell of the fruit.

10. Describe these sensations as you listen to the sounds you make chewing the apple. What do you notice?

To some people, this may seem like a silly exercise, something without purpose, even weird. But if you've done it—not just read about it, but actually done it—you now know what losing your mind and coming to your senses is. It's a way of turning off the mental drone and hum that often intensifies our fears and, instead, opening up to simpler ways of experiencing the world.

I'm sure you've heard people say that little kids and dogs can really sense whether you like them or not. In fact, they are often more on target than educated adults. How do you think they can zero in on people's feelings like that? It's not by means of intellectual thinking. It's by being aware of what their senses are telling them. Young children's uncluttered minds allow them a clarity of perception that often eludes older children and adults, whose minds are full of assumptions, preconceptions, and analytical processes that may actually confuse matters.

Have an Out-of-Body Experience

To acquire knowledge, one must study; but to acquire wisdom, one must observe.

—MARILYN VOS SAVANT

If you're capable of stepping outside of yourself to observe your fear, you've taken a big stride forward.

Kelly knew that she was making good progress toward taming her fears when she said to me, "I've developed the ability to have an out-of-body experience with my fears. It's hard to describe, but I'll try. It's like I used to be at the mercy of my fears. They'd come, they'd conquer, they'd vanquish me. But now, when my fears come, I not only feel them, I also observe them, I label them, I describe them, I evaluate them. I'm a witness to my own fear. I can see how they're affecting me. Although I'm not always a happy camper, I'm also no longer a defeated victim, and that makes me feel very good."

She went on to say, "I can also get in touch with the stronger, more secure part of me, which is usually hanging around somewhere in the background. This part of me is supportive and reassuring. It kind of acts like a nurturing parent and tells me I'll be okay. I know now that I don't have to listen to my fears or be overcome by them. I can acknowledge them but focus instead on whatever I need to do to get beyond them."

Or, as Ivy said, "I have a fear that I call buyer's remorse. Shortly after I purchase an item—it could be anything from a coat to a car—I can get very panicky. Somehow, even if I loved the item when I bought it, I become convinced that I've made the most dreadful mistake. I used to give myself such a hard time. But now it's such a familiar fear that even though I feel it, I can also chuckle to myself, and say, uh-oh—buyer's remorse. Here we go again. But I know the feeling will pass. Don't tell my husband this, but it actually reminds me of PMS. The feelings are intense. I don't have much control over them. But once I recognize what's happening, I can put things in perspective more easily, knowing that in a few days, I really will feel better."

Helping yourself by becoming a third-party observer works regardless of *how* you feel the fear—whether your mind has gone blank, you're on pins and needles, you're sweating bullets, you feel jittery, you're intimidated, you're overwhelmed, or you're panicky. I'm sure you've actually experienced something similar regarding one emotion or another at some point in your life. Perhaps you've been acting silly, and your third-party observer lets you know. You might think to yourself, "Gee, I'm real zany tonight." You're not passing judgment on yourself, and you're not stopping the behavior; you're just aware of how you're conducting yourself. You're mindful of what's happening, and you know it's not the worst thing to do. (If it *were* getting out of hand, this observant part of you will protect you and help you modify your response by telling you, "Hey, you're no longer silly—now you're acting like an idiot!")

Fear of Flying

Alexandra, who exhibits both a Compliant and a Hypervigilant fear style, has always been a nervous flier. Although she dreads air travel, her work demands that she take occasional trips. Thus, she has no recourse but to tolerate the situation. During a red-eye flight from Los Angeles to New York City, Alexandra felt something tighten in her gut when the captain's voice came on over the loudspeaker. "Folks, ground control has alerted us to the likelihood of turbulence a few hours ahead. Please keep your seat belts fastened so the flight attendants won't have to wake you up midflight."

Alexandra observed herself getting upset in response to the captain's message. "Uh-oh," she told herself, "I hope this plane doesn't crash. I hope I can live to see my kids grow up." As her thoughts started to spiral out of control, she took a deep breath. "Whoa, girl, calm down. You don't like what's happening. You're scared. But the captain had such a comforting voice—he wasn't at all nervous about the turbulence, was he? And he's the one in charge." Alexandra had always been someone who felt comforted by people in authority if they seemed sincere and confident. Their authoritative strength made her feel calmer, more relaxed. She remembered how, as a child, she would turn to her dad whenever she felt scared. At those times he'd tell her, "Don't be afraid. I'm going to be here, and I'm not going to let anything happen to my little girl." Already she began to feel better.

Then another thought popped into her head: "I've never heard any captain or flight attendant predict turbulence hours before we reach it." Just knowing that the ground control personnel could predict the situation now seemed to reassure her. She felt herself becoming more at ease, as she told herself, "I always believed that turbulence was a surprise. The plane suddenly hits rough air, it catches the pilot off guard, and he struggles to keep the plane steady. But if the captain can predict these conditions several hours in advance, maybe it's no big deal—maybe for them it's nothing more than a bumpy road that they warn us about so that *we* don't panic."

Alexandra, whose mind easily goes on overload, soon began to equate turbulence with bumpy, then bumpy with a kiddie roller-coaster ride, which reminded her of the fun she'd had at an amusement park with her five-year-old just a week earlier. She had never been someone who enjoyed an adult roller coaster; that scared her half to death. But a kiddie ride was another matter—something she could actually enjoy. So when the turbulence did occur, Alexandra closed her eyes, breathed deeply, and pretended she was on a kiddie roller coaster. As she did so, white-knuckle dread turned into something that felt more like excitement and fun—an adventure. It seemed crazy to her that she could make this transition, but she did.

As the Roman poet Horace wrote, "Remember when life's path is steep to keep your mind level."

7

Steps for Enhancing Your Language

Sticks and stones will break my bones, but words will never harm me.

WRONG, WRONG, WRONG!

The words you use to express yourself have a big influence on your fears—sometimes in positive ways, more often in negative ways. The same is true of the words you hear others say about you. If you grew up hearing wonderful words—"You're terrific," "I'm so proud of you," "I'm sure you'll succeed"—the world you experience is far different than if you heard, "You're such a loser," "You're hopeless," or "You'll never amount to anything." And if you use encouraging words when you're speaking about yourself—"I'll do my best" or "I'm going to get that job"—you'll live a far different life than if you say, "I just can't do it," or "I don't know why anyone would choose me." Words may not break your bones, but they sure can burden your mind and crush your spirit.

How Your Words Influence
Your State of Mind

One comes to believe whatever one repeats to oneself sufficiently often, whether the statement be true or false. It comes to be the dominating thought in one's mind.

—ROBERT COLLIER

People typically use words without any awareness of how this can intensify or diminish their fears. This happens out of habit, not by choice. Unwittingly, you may find that you're your own worst enemy, creating fear by your choice of words, even terrifying yourself when it would be so much better if you could be calming yourself. In this chapter, you'll learn to expand your word choices, minimizing melodramatic and histrionic language that serves no useful purpose, and embracing language that reassures, empowers, and maybe even inspires you.

Language can pack a punch. Make it work for you!

Language—Marc's Downward Slide

"I can't do it any more!" Marc cried in frustration. For two years he had worked as a manager for a carpet store, and for most of that time he wished he had a better job. "I don't like this work, but I don't know what else to do," he complained. "It makes me so tense, thinking about how frustrated I am in this job, and yet I'm afraid to leave it."

Soon afterward, Marc heard of a possible managerial position at a computer software company. He was pleased. "Wouldn't it be great if I could have a job I really loved?" he asked, smiling.

Three weeks later, though, Marc was back to chanting his *I can't/I don't know* mantra.

"What happened?" I asked.

He shrugged. "I went for the interview, but I was too nervous to do my best. As soon as they asked me the first question, I got uptight.

It didn't go well at all. If I were the interviewer, even *I* wouldn't have hired me."

Poor Marc had undermined himself once again with his negativity. His choice of language (especially his frequent use of "I can't" and "I don't know") created a classic self-fulfilling prophecy. His words made him feel helpless, stupid, and frustrated, with precious little energy for optimism or a forward-thinking attitude.

Although you can't undo the words you heard long ago, you can make sure that the words you use today—to yourself as well as others—will inspire, encourage, motivate, and validate. Upbeat but realistic statements will help you keep up your spirit, nourish your optimism, and reduce your fears. Too often, other people—even well-meaning people—either give negative evaluations (labeling, criticizing, or ridiculing) or maintain silence instead of saying something supportive.

Of course, you can't control what other people say to you or about you; you can, however, control what you say to yourself. Think about how much better you'd feel if you never missed an opportunity to tell yourself (when appropriate) what a good job you did. And when you didn't do a good job, think how much better you'd feel if you told yourself that you admire your courage for trying anyway, and for learning from the experience. It's no exaggeration to say that changing your language can change your life.

It's also possible, depending on your choice of words, to set a negative cycle in motion that intensifies rather than calms your fears. If you are afraid, your voice may be hesitant, timid, or silent. When you do speak, you will likely do so in a manner that *maximizes* your fear and *minimizes* your confidence. The following are some ways that this process happens.

Magnifying Your Fear with "Trigger Words"

Trigger words are words that instantly spark your fear. Say them and, lickety-split, your muscles tighten up, your heart pounds, and your mouth gets dry as you start to anticipate the worst. These words undermine your confidence and intensify your doubts. Here's a checklist of some trigger words, plus extra space for you to write down your own fear phrases.

- I can't deal with this.
- I don't know anything about this.
- I'm so stupid.
- I'm such an idiot.
- I'll never be able to cope with this.
- I'm dead from the neck up.
- My ideas are half-baked.
- It's way too difficult for me.
- I'm a ditz.
- I always screw up.
- Whatever I do turns out wrong.

Can you think of other trigger words or phrases that you use?

1. _____

2. _____

3. _____

Making the Problem Bigger than Life

Here are dramatic phrases that turn an unusual (or even routine) situation into an enormous problem. Some examples include:

- It's the worst thing that could have happened!
- This is a total disaster!
- It's devastating!
- It's a catastrophe!
- Oh my God! Oh my God! Oh my God!
- It's dreadful!
- It's beyond anything I could ever imagine!
- Things will never be the same!
- This is unbelievably terrible!

In addition to exaggerating the problem, these words reduce the power of the problem solver. Are there other words or phrases you use that make your problems seem larger than life?

1. _____

2. _____

3. _____

Intensifying Your Reaction to the Situation

Similarly, the way you talk to yourself about your reaction will intensify your fears as well as weaken your ability to cope. These are words like:

- I'll never recover!
- I'll never get over this!
- I'm completely blown away!
- I'll never trust anybody ever again!
- What's the point in going on?
- I'm in shock!
- I'm terrified!
- I'm filled with dread!
- I'm scared to death!

What are some statements you use that may intensify your reaction to situations you need to face?

1. _____

2. _____

3. _____

Turning Fear Talk into Calming Talk

In contrast, it's also possible to set a positive cycle in motion—a cycle in which thoughts, words, and actions reinforce one another to free you from the debilitating aspects of fear. I strongly believe that speaking in upbeat ways can be the easiest way to start the change process. Why? Because it's easy to say something without fully meaning it at first. You can simply "try it on for size" just as you might try out a new fashion you're not sure you'll like, then see how it feels. With this approach there's no harm done; you can take a crack at voicing a new attitude without risk, then see what happens. Since language can be such a powerful influence on how you perceive yourself and how others perceive you, I urge you to try out the following exercises, which many of my patients have found beneficial.

All fear sentences have an opposite. The flip side of the coin can get you in touch with your competence, help you maintain a perspective, and moderate your reaction to the situation. Here are three examples of fear talk and matched examples of calming talk that can counteract your fear.

Fear talk: I can't deal with this.
Calming talk: I can deal with this.

Fear talk: It's the worst thing that could have happened.
Calming talk: It's not the worst thing that could have happened.

Fear talk: I'll never recover from this.
Calming talk: I will be able to recover from this.

However, sometimes when you "try on" the opposite phrase to see how it fits, you think, "No way, this just isn't true." No problem. In these situations, what you may need is a modified response, rather than the exact opposite of the fear-causing phrase. Here are a few examples:

Fear talk: I can't deal with this.
Calming talk: It's going to be tough for me to deal with this, but I know someone who can help me. (This could be a spouse, a friend, a psychologist, or some other professional adviser.)

Fear talk: It's the worst thing that could have happened.
Calming talk: This is a really bad thing that has happened, but I won't let it destroy me.

Fear talk: I'll never recover from this.
Calming talk: It will take me a long time to recover from this, but I expect that I can eventually put it behind me.

Notice that fear phrases are often short and generalized. Calming phrases, on the other hand, are longer and often have two aspects to them. One aspect is a modified version of the fear statement; the other aspect is a more hopeful personal statement that promotes competence, safety, or recovery. Why do we use the scarier words? For Mario, it was simply a habit; that's the way he heard his father speak, so that's the way he spoke. Others are seduced by the drama of it. A more moderated word may seem dull, whereas a more dramatic word seems momentous.

I suggest that you experiment with turning fear words into calming words. In the following spaces, write one of your fear words or phrases, then try out other phrases that offer you more hopeful alternatives in your patterns of speech.

Fear words: _____

Calming words: _____

Developing Your Own Voice

Few kids today are raised by the old adage "Children should be seen and not heard." Indeed, many modern families are so child-centered that the children are heard more than the adults. Nevertheless, some people still grow up without a voice. They listen. They obey. They acquiesce. When told to jump, they ask how high. They don't ask themselves, "What do I think?" but rather "What am I *supposed* to think?" Without self-dialogue, they don't have the skills even to think about what they think.

"I can communicate well with people if we're working together on a structured project," says Lisa, a Shy woman who has struggled with the issue of not having a voice. "But I get apprehensive and have no idea what to say to people when we're just socializing. I didn't grow up around much talking. In our family, my sister and I just *listened* to our parents. We didn't disagree with them or add our points of view— if we knew we had one! That would have been grounds for a lecture on how fresh and ungrateful we were—and maybe a smack across the face. And I certainly wasn't able to speak to anyone outside my family about problems or ideas. That would have been treasonous, since you didn't air your dirty laundry in public. Even my sister and I didn't talk much to each other."

These day-to-day family dynamics damaged Lisa's ability to communicate with others. Her parents' discipline methods made the problem worse. "Though I hated my father's physical abuse, I felt even worse when my mother punished me. She'd cut me off and not talk to me for days. Like I wasn't worth wasting her time on." Among the results of this really bad parenting was that Lisa silenced herself as well. She never believed that what she thought, felt, or said really mattered.

In recent years, however, Lisa has succeeded in making significant changes. "I'm just now beginning to realize that I should have a voice, an opinion, and that my ideas might count for something. I've begun to keep a journal. I think it's a kind of silent voice. I have the freedom to put whatever I'm thinking into words. Some day I'll have the courage to read my journal out loud and actually hear my words, but I'm not ready for that yet."

Like most change, Lisa's transformation was gradual. She used to believe (as is true of many women raised before the days of feminism) that she should rely on authority for the "truth," and that authority was invariably a male voice. However, Lisa began to change her assumptions as she became friendly with more outspoken women. One in particular, a neighbor, often told Lisa how smart she was— something that Lisa hadn't really considered before. But the biggest change occurred as a result of a child-rearing crisis with her husband, Al. The couple's sons, ages six and eight, squabbled a lot. Lisa felt that the boys' disagreements were ordinary sibling rivalry. Al, however, had complicated and unrealistic theories about child development. When Lisa listened closely to his ideas about how they should behave, she realized how much of his talk was full of hot air. He knew little about children, but that didn't stop him from expounding his views in a pompous and opinionated manner. In contrast, she noticed how quiet she was—despite a lot more knowledge, knowledge she'd gained from reading, from discussing these issues with friends, and from taking parenting courses. She began to realize that instead of always being passive and listening to others, she should have an active voice and trust what she knew.

Many people have experiences like Lisa's, in which they weren't encouraged to have their own voice. Others struggle with even more traumatic experiences, such as sexual abuse, which may silence any ability to protest or even describe what has happened. Young people, especially, don't have the words to describe traumatic experiences. Feeling helpless, defenseless, and overwhelmed, they may conclude that the problem is their own fault. This self-blame may silence them further. In reality, silence may be the safest way for a child living under difficult circumstances to survive. As an adult, however, silence is often unnecessary.

Have you had difficulty developing your own voice? If so, I hope there will be a safe time and place for you to talk about what happened to you. I hope you will be heard and feel validated and understood. By telling your story, you honor what you have endured. By contrast, *not* talking about a difficult or traumatic experience—and thus continuing to silence your voice—compounds the problem. If you're unable to express what has happened to you, there's a tendency to feel isolated from others, then to feel alienated from them, because they don't understand what you've gone through. To make matters worse, you probably don't fully comprehend your own experiences either.

"As a young boy," Jerome states, "one of my uncles repeatedly molested me. I thought I'd brought this situation on myself, and I felt so ashamed about these experiences that I never told a soul about them. But because of the growing openness about sex abuse in recent years, I finally found the courage to confide to one of my brothers about what happened. His response was, 'It happened to me, too.' That shocked me! I wondered how many others also got molested and never spoke up?" Jerome discovered that confiding in a trusted person started the healing process.

Ways to Find Your Own Voice

How can you find your voice? Here are some methods I recommend:

- Create quiet time alone to think, ponder, meditate, or pray.

- Set aside a place that's your own territory (a room, a place

within a room, or some other private space) in order to hear
your voice.

- Develop a friendship with a compassionate person who will
  respect and encourage your voice.

- Ask yourself refective questions and answer them, keeping in
  mind that there's no right or wrong answer, only your opinion.
  (What would I do if I won the lottery? What do I want to discuss with my child's teacher? What do I think about the lead
  story in the newspaper?)

- Participate actively in a conversation. Allow yourself the right
  to your own opinion, even if it's not an expert opinion.

- Keep a journal so that you can record, reread, and contemplate
  your thoughts (and the progress of your thinking) over a
  period of time.

- Tell your story to a psychologist or another person willing and
  able to listen with understanding and compassion.

- Derive new meaning from your story as you tell it. Explaining
  what happened to you provides an opportunity to learn new
  lessons about life as well as reach new insights about yourself.

- Let yourself feel whatever emotions you feel. You don't need to
  understand or evaluate the emotions; just let them be.

Your story is as unique as your fingerprints. It is precious—even
the painful part is precious—because it has made you *you*. Telling
your story in your own words is essential. It is not sweeping your
experiences under the rug, pretending they didn't happen. It is not
minimizing your experiences, trying to convince yourself that
they weren't so bad. It is not exaggerating your experiences, making
yourself into a perennial victim. It's simply telling what happened
to you—its meaning, its consequences, and how it affects you
today. The healing that comes from this process can be absolutely
amazing.

Sometimes describing an experience is difficult because you can't
find the right terminology to explain what you've been through. Keep
in mind that the struggle to find the words doesn't mean the problem

is your fault. Sometimes you just don't know how to explain it. Sometimes the vocabulary doesn't even exist yet. When our society finally grapples with a subject that has great emotional impact, new words are often invented to help explain the syndrome.

Here are some words and phrases that are relatively new concepts:

- Ageism
- Bipolar disorder
- Borderline personality
- Children of Holocaust survivors
- Date rape
- Domestic violence
- Dysfunctional families
- Emotional abuse
- Family systems
- Mood disorder
- Parental neglect
- Passive-aggressive behavior
- Racism
- Rageaholic
- Sexism

Some of these terms, such as sexism, weren't to be found in older dictionaries. Others, such as mood disorder, existed but weren't part of common parlance. Before these terms existed, many vulnerable people had no idea how to describe their experiences. Even though they had firsthand knowledge of what happened to them, they needed the language to help them understand their ordeals. Words help us comprehend that *"this* is what happened" rather than having a vague, hazy idea that "I'm not sure what happened." (An example of this issue is the recent stories about sexual abuse by priests.) Many accounts illustrate that people wrestle with what they have experienced, particularly during childhood—and often doubt the reality of their ordeals—until they can speak openly about them.

Fear—and Silence

Another way we may silence our voice is by being passive or too accepting. The following is a personal example. During the early1960's, I applied to graduate schools and was turned down by most because they had a quota, accepting very few women applicants. When asked in interviews if I intended to marry and have children, I responded with an honest yes. The result was a closed door. Was I angry about these sexist policies? Absolutely not. I wasn't smart enough to be angry. Instead, I bought into the administrators' rationale that I would be taking a spot away from a man who would need it more than I did. I'd have a man to support me. Did those closed doors generate fear in me? Definitely. I felt apprehension that I'd have no role in society other than wife and mother; I felt dismay that I couldn't fulfill my goals; and I felt anxiety that I wasn't good enough. In those days, I wasn't a fighter for my rights (and even today, I'm pretty much a pussycat) but, in my favor, I don't give up easily. Eventually I was accepted to Temple University, where they not only welcomed me, they also provided me with generous financial support.

Self-Talk that Increases Your Fears

The way you speak to others is important, but it's not nearly as significant as the way you speak to yourself. You'd think that if you had an opportunity to have an internal dialogue, you'd pick out the best words to say—words that would make you feel pleased, safe, and happy. After all, no one is barking at you to do this or that. No one is berating you for what you did wrong. You can say anything you want. Yet many of us have unending internal dialogues—what I call self-talk—that serves no purpose except to make ourselves miserable. And often the misery is intertwined with fear.

The following are some ways that self-talk can be negative and fear-oriented.

Telling Yourself that the Situation Is Awful

Many people remember only the negative part of a situation to the exclusion of everything else. But when you focus only on the negative, it's easy to magnify what's bad. You fill your mind with depressing thoughts, which can make the whole experience (even a good one) a downer. Take the example of a pleasant vacation marred by a few days of rain or a delayed flight. Do you have a tendency to describe such setbacks as awful, saying such things as, "The weather ruined the vacation," or "The flight was so long, it hardly even paid to go."

Carl received a "piss-poor rating" (in his words) on his last job evaluation. He felt tortured. "I go right into fear mode," he says. "I'm relentless in my self-criticism. I think everything is wrong with me and I'm very hard on myself. This job isn't such a great one to begin with, and I can't even do this one well! I'll never make it in this world." He goes on to describe his situation as thoroughly awful. "I'm approaching forty. When I look at my peers and see how much more they have than I do, the anxiety comes rushing in. My self-confidence goes out the window. I feel disconnected, depressed, miserable, and convinced I'll never get a break." But when Carl showed his wife the evaluation, she didn't think it was nearly as bad as he did. She pointed out that Carl's supervisor had highlighted his strengths as well as areas in which he needs improvement. When Carl read it over a second time, the report didn't seem quite as bad as when he'd initially read it. He recognized that most of the criticisms were of things he could easily improve, like late reports and excessive absences. Gradually Carl started to see the situation as less than awful. "I know I tend to think everything is dreadful," he noted, "when in reality it's often just a disappointment or a temporary setback."

Talk of Impending Doom

Vivian, who is Hypervigilant and Controlling, comes from a family in which both of her parents were alcoholic. During her childhood, she never knew what could happen. Things might be calm at one moment, then all hell would break loose. Now she sees danger everywhere and worries about everything. "I'm especially concerned about my kids. My primary responsibility is to keep them safe. Actually, I'd like to keep them on a leash—in my sight all the time. I was always watching out for them when they were younger, but now that they're older, it's harder for me. I'm torn between letting them grow up, which I know they need to do, and desperately wanting to keep them safe."

Vivian feels so afraid that she's sometimes out of control. She can go bonkers with the kids when they want to do something that she regards as dangerous, such as leaving the suburbs and venturing into the city, or even visiting a friend of a friend who lives just minutes away. "I have a radius of safety—the town I live in and the three surrounding towns. Beyond that, everything feels like a foreign country. I feel threatened if I don't know the area. It feels unsafe. Anything can happen there."

The trickiest situation facing her at the moment is that her seventeen-year-old son, Ian, wants to visit a college that he may apply to. A friend's brother goes there, so Ian would like to spend a weekend in the dorm with the two guys. That sounds harmless, yet Vivian feels deeply fearful about this possible arrangement. "My mind goes right away to what's potentially risky about this arrangement. Who is the friend's brother, and who else might be there? How do I know they'll drive carefully? Will they get my kid drunk or stoned? Or exclude him from the action? Or maybe lose him?" Vivian's self-talk quickly puts her into a tizzy. Ironically, it's her son who helps her put these situations into perspective. "My son is just the opposite of me— a very laid back, relaxed kid. He's always telling me to chill out; there's nothing to worry about. I wish some of his easygoing nature could rub off on me!"

Softening Your Harsh Inner Critic

With a relentless inner critic, you may blame yourself for things that actually have little or nothing to do with you, such as thinking you're a terrible parent because your child was disrespectful toward a teacher. You may end up obsessing about what you did wrong rather than what you did right. Even when events are directly your fault, you may still overpersonalize, saying, "I made such stupid mistakes," rather than just accepting that things didn't go well that day.

Each of us has an inner critic, and that's not necessarily a problem. But if your inner critic pounces on you, attacks you, and tortures you like an enemy, *that's* a problem. Diane, who is Hypervigilant, exemplifies this situation. "If I do something that didn't work out right, I don't simply say I made a mistake. I go beyond that and tell myself that I'm a moron. I know I shouldn't, but I do. I can't help it. It's like I do my own character assassination."

It's very important for you to minimize this kind of self-criticism. Give yourself a chance to make mistakes like anyone else. Consider that you're in the middle of a process, whatever that may be—you're still learning (to cook, to write, to learn a new job, whatever) and you're still developing as a person. By toning down your self-criticism, you'll not only give yourself some leeway, you'll also diminish your fears. Don't magnify dangers or problems. Don't make your life more complicated or stressful than it already is. Make a habit of saying positive things about yourself—and to yourself. If you want to moderate the power of your inner critic, here are some more ways.

Accept your weaknesses. We've all got them, although some folks brag about them while others conceal them. Either way is okay. All I'm asking you to do is to accept that you have not only weaknesses, but flaws, deficiencies, and shortcomings. Then ask yourself, so what? It doesn't make you a bad person or a stupid one. If your weakness bothers you, you have the option of correcting it or refining it with some serious effort. Even if you feel like you have two left hands, you can learn to cook, dance, write, speak, paint, even pilot an airplane. You may never reach an expert level, maybe not even an intermediate one, but you can certainly increase your know-how.

Speak more compassionately about your shortcomings. If you hate to make a mistake, perhaps the words you use can help you take it in stride. Would it be easier for you if you admitted to miscalculating those numbers, misinterpreting someone's intentions, omitting a certain step, overlooking that detail, underestimating someone's resistance, or overestimating a person's kindness? Or how about just fessing up that you goofed, or coming clean that you messed up? By changing the words you use, are you playing a con game with yourself? Is all of this just semantics? Or is it, as I believe, a more precise and kinder interpretation of your mistakes?

Minimize your self-criticism. Have you ever been on a diet where you decided to cut down on high-calorie food? Now it's time to take the same approach to self-criticism. Use this prescription: ingest no more than one or two bits of criticism each day. More than that is an overdose. And while you're at it, how about toning down not only the *frequency* of the self-criticism but also the *dosage*? The most effective therapeutic dose is always the lowest level that works. Cut yourself some slack. Give yourself a break. Make a habit of saying something nice about yourself every single day.

ALTERNATIVES TO SELF-CRITICISM

An occasional compliment is necessary to keep up one's self-respect. When you cannot get a compliment any other way, pay yourself one.

—MARK TWAIN

- Instead of saying, "I did it all wrong, " say, "Maybe there's room for improvement, but I did well under the circumstances."

- Instead of saying, "My presentation was a fiasco," say, "Like everything else, my presentation had its pluses and minuses."

- Instead of saying, "Why did I make those stupid comments?" say, "I could have chosen my words better, but there's probably no harm done."

- Instead of saying, "I totally messed up," say, "I made some mistakes, but now I've learned what I can do better."

- Instead of saying, "He isn't satisfied with me," say, "You can't please everyone, but I'm satisfied with what I did."

You don't need to be your toughest critic. Trust me, there will always be someone out there who's willing to do that job for you. Be more compassionate to yourself—at least as patient, understanding, and kind as you'd be toward a good friend.

More Verbal Strategies

You now have a better understanding of how your choice of language can reduce your fears. Here are a few more strategies that work well.

Avoid Shoulds and Have-to's

Just as the mere smell of food can create an urge to eat, so can a simple word or words create a fear response. Here's what I mean. Complete this sentence as though it applies to you: I should

_____.

Let's say you wrote, "I should do a better job keeping the house clean."

Now let's see how a single word change can make a difference. Keep that same sentence but change "I should" to "I could," so that your sentence reads "I could do a better job keeping the house clean." What is the effect of this one simple change? Almost invariably the result is less intensity, less harshness, less fear. There's more calm, more choice, more acceptance.

There's something tyrannical about the word *should*; it tells you you're not doing enough, you didn't measure up. What's the matter with you? You're not complying! You didn't do what you were supposed to do! The word *should* creates pressure, increases tension, and creates an albatross around your neck. Why? Because *should* is an authoritarian word that represents your parent, your teacher, or society telling you what to do. You find yourself in the role of the child. Are you measuring up? Are you doing what you're supposed to do? Are you obeying the rules? If not, you've failed your duty and obligation.

By contrast, the word *could* is far less authoritarian, far less fear-inducing. When you say *I could*, you place yourself in the role of the adult. You can make choices. You can do A, B, C, or even D. Or you can do A at a later date, do A partially but not fully, or else say A but not do A. All of these options become possibilities when you use *I could* rather than *I should*.

Are you ready to give up the tyranny of your shoulds? I hope so. Demanding words like *should* can make taming your fears more difficult. Here's your opportunity to change your *shoulds* to *coulds*.

Should Message   Could Message

1. _____   1. _____

2. _____   2. _____

3. _____   3. _____

4. _____   4. _____

What have you discovered from this exercise?

A similar pattern holds true with "have to" sentences. "Have to" exerts pressure and allows you few or no options. Write a sentence that begins with "I have to": I have to _____.

Now write the same sentence but change "I have to" to "I want to." Notice how the change affects your view of the situation. Suppose you wrote, "I have to spend more time with my kids." As with phrasing that uses "I should," "I have to" leaves you no element of choice; it increases the pressure on you and squashes your creative thinking. But when you change your *have to* to *want to*, you can hear your real message: "I want to spend more time with my kids." This phrasing can lead to better decision making.

Another advantage to saying "I want to" instead of "I have to" is that you'll recognize more about what you really do want. If your sentence was, "I have to go to my awful job" and you change it to say, "I want to go to my awful job," insights may crystallize in your mind. "No," you tell yourself, "I *don't* want to go my awful job. What I really want is to find a better job." Then other questions arise. "How can I do that? What type of job would bring me more satisfaction?" Such questions are complex and often difficult to answer. But at least your questions start to advance the process. Your orientation is now directed toward finding a solution, not simply complaining about what you have to do. Here is your opportunity to put this strategy into practice.

I *have* to

1. _____
2. _____
3. _____
4. _____

I *want* to

1. _____
2. _____
3. _____
4. _____

Maintaining a Perspective

Dwelling on the negative simply contributes to its power.

—Shirley MacLaine

Marlene habitually describes every bothersome experience as a disaster. "The cruise was *awful!*" she exclaims. "The baggage people misplaced one of our suitcases for six hours and I was afraid they'd never find it. The air conditioning shut off several times and I could barely breathe. The weather was dreadful. And I thought I'd die from being so seasick. By the time it was all over, I felt so fed up I could practically scream!" Perhaps she had a right to her frustrations by describing her trip as the worst maritime disaster since the sinking of the *Titanic*. Still, her words contributed to making her vacation far more miserable than it would have been otherwise.

It's remarkable how often we speak of routine events in catastrophic language. True, life is full of problems. The car won't start. The cat messes up the carpet. Your child skins a knee. A friend takes offense at your remarks. But do these mishaps, and even more serious crises, really warrant the doom-and-gloom utterances that many of us tend to use?

Most people experience only a very few catastrophic events during their lifetimes, yet catastrophic language abounds. Without intending to (or without even being aware of what we're doing), we use intense, alarming, fear-inducing language. These "Oh my God!"

phrases, as I call them, heighten your reactions to events, and limit your ability to cope with whatever is happening. Your choice of words can make you think that an extreme, monstrous, unbearable event has happened, but the chances are that the situation is far from being so terrible. Most problems can be solved. Most mistakes can be corrected. Most illnesses can be treated. Getting fired can be an opportunity for a better job. A divorce can be a new start in life. I don't mean to trivialize major happenings, yet I believe that you're better off if you avoid attributing extreme and terrible consequences to life events, even serious life events. Extreme utterances don't diminish your fear; on the contrary, they pour gasoline on the fire.

You've probably noticed that at truly catastrophic times, words seem meaningless and empty. What we cherish at those times are a caring hand and a loving embrace. We want to touch another human being; we don't want to hear a lot of words. If you've witnessed a horrible event, as did the air traffic controllers who realized before anyone else what was happening on the morning of September 11, there is usually complete silence; talking comes later. For other observers, reactions on that sunny morning were simply, "Oh my God, oh my God, oh my God" or "No, no no!" The words we utter during truly catastrophic times are short and simple.

I recommend you keep your words in proportion to the problems you're experiencing. If you've suffered a genuine tragedy, you have every right to intense expressions of grief, sadness, and anguish. But if you're dealing with ordinary mishaps—dropping a bag of groceries, missing a bus, locking your keys in the car, or having your phone service interrupted—don't intensify your fears and frustration by overstating what has happened to you.

8

Steps for Transforming Your Speech Patterns

JUST AS IT'S CRUCIAL TO AVOID certain speech patterns that intensify fear, it's also important to emphasize certain patterns that promote confidence. Speaking in decisive, upbeat ways can bolster your courage and help you tame your fears. It's not even necessary at first to feel the confidence and strength of your uplifting words; sometimes it just starts the process while the feelings come later.

Change How You Describe Your Fear

The language you use to describe your fear will have a strong influence on how you view yourself and your situation.

Here's a simple example. Read these three statements:

- I'm a fearful [or anxious, scared] person.
- I'm always afraid.
- I'll be afraid the rest of my life.

Now compare the first three statements with the next three:

- I've been afraid recently.
- Sometimes I feel afraid.
- I'm afraid.

In one sense, all of the statements are the same: you're describing yourself as afraid. However, the first three are much more pessimistic and self-defeating than the last three. Here's why.

I'm a fearful person labels your whole personality and presents yourself to the world with a sign around your neck marked *fearful*. You overidentify with your fear, making it the primary feature of who you are and what you're about. It's ironic that most people hate it when others label them, yet many don't hesitate to label themselves in a derogatory manner.

I'm always afraid is a discouraging statement that can become a self-fulfilling prophecy. This is absolute, all-or-nothing thinking at its worst. Even the most fearful person I know doesn't feel afraid a hundred percent of the time. When you describe yourself in that manner, you discount the times when you feel all right, and you overlook the more serene moments in life.

I'll be afraid for the rest of my life is perhaps the most definitive way to stay stuck in your fear forever. With this rigid choice of words, you close off the future to any new possibilities.

Now consider how the second set of statements differs from the first set. These three statements don't sugarcoat anything. You acknowledge that you're afraid, but you don't exaggerate your state of mind, nor do you blame or label yourself in a negative way. You also assume that there can be future times in which you won't feel so afraid. Let's look at these statements one at a time.

I've been afraid recently implicitly asks the question Why? You search for what has been happening recently in your relationships, your career, your body, or your mind that may have brought about or aggravated your fear. You believe that fear won't take up residence in your brain. You keep the door open to changing your emotional state.

Sometimes I feel afraid is a statement recognizing that emotions come and emotions go. At times you feel afraid; at other times you don't. You don't view fearfulness as an absolute or permanent condition in your life. This comment is much more hopeful than many of the others.

I'm afraid is the simplest statement of all. You acknowledge your condition of the moment without assuming that it's a feature of your character or that it will haunt you for any length of time. Maybe you're afraid because you're switching from one job to another, because a relationship has ended, or because you're moving to a new city. It's temporary in the same way that "I'm tired" or "I'm hungry" is temporary. Even if the situation is more serious or troubling, you don't initially alarm yourself by assuming things are more threatening than they really are.

Decide Whose Voice You'll Listen To

During childhood, so many people tell you so many things that their words may have a cumulative effect. Maybe your big brother always called you a fool. Or your sister called you a ditz. Or your mother's remarks were constantly critical. Or your father told you in no uncertain terms that you were too sensitive and that you should toughen up. Because you heard those messages repeated many times, and because you heard them when you were young and vulnerable, you probably still hear those voices echoing in your mind. Although those messages may seem to belong to another era, they may still have sufficient power to inspire fear in you now.

If you give a lot of importance to the negative voices, it's likely that you won't hear the more positive ones. For instance, it's likely that for every person who thought you were too sensitive, there were twice as many who appreciated your sensitivity. For every person who thought you could do nothing right, there were probably many more who admired your skills and knowledge.

So the crucial question is: Whose voice will you listen to? I urge you to listen to the voices that help you develop your confidence. The ones that build your backbone. The ones that you respect the most. The ones that are true in today's context.

For every aphorism, there's another that asserts just the opposite. Which one is right? "A stitch in time saves nine," or "Haste makes waste"? "Opposites attract," or "Birds of a feather flock together"? These sayings, although contradictory, may both be good advice; it all depends on the context. The same holds true for comments that people make about you. For this reason, make sure that the voice you listen to is one that's helpful at this time, in this context. It should never be the totally critical voice, the one that puts you down or humiliates you. However, it may be one that offers constructive criticism, in a reassuring manner, not a hostile one. It won't suggest, "You're a screwup—you slur your words and speak so fast that nobody understands a word you're saying." Rather, it will suggest, "Try not to rush your words. Take your time, calm down, and people will understand you better."

Eva, a patient of mine who made extraordinary progress in her therapy, once confided in me that when her mother said, "Don't go to college," Eva knew instantly that she had to go. Sometimes a person's voice can actually help you decide what to do by prompting you *not* to listen. It could be that you're acting out of defiance, or it could be that you realize that his or her way isn't your way. Eva's mom didn't believe in higher education for girls. Eva did. Whose voice should she have listened to?

If you had to choose whose voice will accompany you through your life, whose would you choose?

Exercise: Listening to the Right Voice for You

1. Write down the name of the person you'd choose to listen to.

   _____

2. Now write what you'd want to hear this person say to you.

   _____

   _____

   _____

3. Why would those words be important to you?

   _____

   _____

   _____

Create a Replacement Strategy

It's not easy to make a negative voice go away just by wishing it wasn't there. Indeed, the more you wish something isn't there, the more you reinforce its presence. Try this example. Take a moment *not* to think of a white elephant standing in the middle of the room. Try really hard not to think of that elephant. What's happening? Paradoxically, the more you try to avoid thinking of the elephant, the longer he hangs around. So what can you do to get rid of those fear-inducing voices that are like elephants making themselves at home in your brain?

The answer is to substitute the voice you don't like with a voice you do. For each fear-inducing voice you hear in your head, replace it with a calm and reassuring one. Sometimes the voice you like will belong to someone you know; at other times, it'll seem to come out of nowhere. Perhaps you've heard the voice in a dream, in a song, or at prayer. It doesn't matter where it comes from. What matters is that you own it. Make it yours. Here's how Amy did just that. Amy's asthma, bronchitis, and allergies interfered with many of the activities she would have liked to participate in. Although she was a good student, she was a nervous child. She remembers her mother referring to her as "my poor Amy" and chatting with her friends about what "a good patient" her daughter was. Because everyone paid so much attention to Amy's breathing problems, her brothers treated her as a victim. Her older brother, Bill, would taunt her, saying, "You're lazy—you get away with everything," while her younger brother, Jack, who felt sorry for her, would say, "You've got it made. You're a girl, so you don't have to worry about being smart."

Amy, who came to therapy when she was twenty-eight years old, is now a healthy young woman. Her illnesses decreased dramatically after she left home. Looking back on her childhood, she concluded that living in a household where both parents smoked and the family owned two cats contributed greatly to her breathing problems. Although she was feeling better physically, her self-image was still in the pits. The labels from her childhood were still ringing in her ears. She viewed herself as lazy, nervous, and jittery, and as a pretty woman who traded on her looks but often felt incompetent.

As she began to feel safe with me, she spoke about her many fears—of not measuring up, of not feeling adequate, of not knowing how to handle herself in social situations. But Amy was willing to stay the course, to learn whatever she needed to learn to feel good about herself and to be more spontaneous with others. Four months later, Amy said, "I remember distinctly the day you told me in that calm, reassuring voice of yours that I'm okay just the way I am. You don't know what that meant to me. I was crying in the car after I left you. Nobody had ever said that to me before."

Since that day, Amy picked up a lot of reassuring messages—from me and from others. The following are the ones that meant the most to her:

- "You're both pretty *and* smart."
- "A mistake isn't the end of the world."
- "You have a good personality and a lot to offer. "
- "A criticism is just a criticism; it's not a judgment of who you are."

Now I'd like you to create your own replacement messages. In the left-hand column, put some messages that you'd like to get out of your head. In the right-hand column, write some messages that you want to get into your head.

Goodbye, Negative Message   Hello, Positive Message

1. _____   1. _____

2. _____   2. _____

3. _____   3. _____

4. _____   4. _____

Delving Deeper into Your Fear

Sometimes we use words not as sources of truth but as quick and easy labels to explain a problem. For instance, we might brand other people as "hysterical," "depressed," "tense," or " anxious." Such words are often overused, becoming simplistic tags that end the process of trying to understand complex personalities. When we slap a label on a person or a problem, we act as though we don't need to look any further for explanations.

For this reason, I recommend that if you're feeling afraid, don't just label your emotion. Instead, explore the feeling by asking and answering questions that will help you become more aware of the deeper meaning of your particular emotional experience. The following are a few suggested questions, plus some space for you to note your responses.

1. How do you feel when you feel afraid? Forget about technical jargon. Just describe your feelings in whatever words seem right for you.

   I feel _____

   _____

2. What else does your fear feel like? Don't stop now—you're just beginning to get started.

   My fear also feels like _____

   _____

3. Stay with your fear and see what images you associate with it. Does this fear remind you of anything you experienced during childhood?

   My fear reminds me of_____

   _____

4. If the event you fear actually occurred, what do you think would happen to you? How would you cope with it?

   I'm worried that this would occur:

   _____

   _____

   And here's how I'd cope with it:

   _____

   _____

5. If you were to use one word or one sound to describe your fear—without censoring yourself—what would it be?

_____

6. Imagine that someone could be there for you when you're feeling so frightened. Whom would you turn to? How could he or she help you?

Here's who I'd want to be present: _____

And here's how he or she could help me:

_____

_____

7. What thoughts easily trigger your fear response?

_____

_____

8. Where in your body do you feel your fear? You may feel the fear in your stomach, chest, head, muscles, or another part of your body.

I feel my fear in these areas: _____

9. Fear may be the feeling you are most aware of, yet there may be other feelings brewing in the background. Are you also feeling sad? Angry? Lonely? Disgusted? Jealous?

Here are my other feelings:

_____

10. Now imagine that you're more aware of the nuances of your fear. What do you know now that you didn't know before?

_____

If you have completed this exercise, I'm sure you have gotten to know your feelings more intimately. You will find this much more helpful than simply labeling yourself as fearful.

Delving Deeper—Alicia's Story

When Alicia asked questions and listened to her answers, here is what she learned about her fear. "My biggest fear is not being able to face the world," said this Shy 32-year-old woman. "I don't know why it's so hard for me, but it is. It seems so easy for others to be with people but for me it's exhausting. I can't relax with others around. I'm always afraid they'll criticize me. My friend Beth says, 'It's no big deal. Just ignore whoever is criticizing you.' But she doesn't know what it's like for me. I just want to curl up and die. It reminds me of my childhood. My parents were always on my case. I felt safe only when I was alone. I wanted to be invisible. It's easier for me to be with one person than to be with a whole group. I'm most relaxed with my husband. He has a nice smile and he knows just what to say to make me feel at ease. I don't want to be dependent on him. I just need him to be there for me and hold me when I'm upset. He can be very comforting—if I let him."

By exploring her fear, Alicia has been able to identify what feelings the fear evokes, how she responds, and what helps her relax. Understanding her fear doesn't automatically make it go away, but it does reduce its intensity and make her feel less alone.

Restating the Problem

Because the English language is so rich in choices, we can express the same thought in many different ways. I'm not suggesting that you lie to yourself or sugarcoat your fears, but do consider how the manner in which you express yourself will influence your emotions and self-assuredness. Using less fear-inducing words will not only lower your fear level, but will also clarify the problem. Minimize the use of words that contribute to your feeling powerless, helpless, passive, or stupid.

Scared to Death—Bella's Story

"My thirteen-year-old daughter Toni is scaring me half to death," says Bella, who tends to be Hypervigilant in her response to fearful situations. "She complains about having chest pains. I don't know whether she's got a heart problem, a breathing problem, or what. I don't know what to do, who to go to, and I'm afraid of what the doctor might find. Maybe she's got a terrible heart condition."

Now consider how Bella might express concerns about her daughter by using less fear-inducing language. " Toni has been complaining about chest pains. I want to have her checked out to see if there's a medical problem or something else. Maybe it's stress, or anxiety, or maybe she's just trying to get out of school. I'm ambivalent about which doctor to see. I'm wavering between her pediatrician, an internist, and a cardiologist. I'm still undecided, but I'll make my decision shortly."

Both of these statements express concern about a potentially serious but ambiguous problem. However, notice how one statement generates doubt, insecurity, and fear, while the other expresses essentially the same issues, but in a more solution-oriented manner. Neither statement sidesteps the issues. The first one, however, gets Bella bogged down in fears that hinder her ability to attend to Toni's health, while the second one clarifies her concerns, helping Bella decide what action to take.

The "What-If" Man

Like many men—especially those who manifest the Macho fear style—Sam avoids going to the doctor because he fears uncovering medical problems he'd rather ignore. "What if the doctor finds something wrong with me?" he wonders. "What if my wife can't count on me because I'm sick? What if I'm a dead man?" These expressions of fear don't provide any answers; they just stoke his worries.

Or consider Jeremy, who's fearful about starting a new job. He asks himself, "What if I fail? What if I don't get along with my coworkers? What if I can't deal with the challenges I'll face?" Once again, these alarming "what if" questions don't lead to a solution; they just leave you twisting in the wind.

A better alternative is to make the "what if" questions into statements. Sam could say, "I'm frightened that the doctor might find something wrong with me. I'd be upset if my wife couldn't depend on me. I worry about having a terminal illness." Or, regarding the job, Jeremy could tell himself, "I'd be so embarrassed if I failed in this new position. I'm concerned about the work relationships I'll have to manage. I'm worried that my responsibilities might be more than I can handle."

Notice what happens when you turn those questions into statements. They don't seem so horrendous, so terrible. Yes, the issues and challenges you face may be serious—they may profoundly challenge your skills or even threaten your life—but as statements rather than questions, they don't leave you hanging with agonizing alarm and dread.

A second alternative is to make the situation less dramatic by actually answering the "what if" questions in a realistic manner. Even with a worst-case scenario, Sam could say, "What if it's cancer? Well, if that's what I've got, I'll have to deal with it. My friend Benjamin knows a top oncologist, so at least I'll know who to go to." As he responds to the other issues that his questions raise, the whole situation, although serious, becomes much less ominous.

The same holds true for Jeremy's job. He can ask, "What if I can't handle this new position?" and then answer his own question: "It'll be a blow to my ego and to our income, but one way or the other, we'll face it. We've got some investments (in part, because we've thought about these risks beforehand). I've responded to similar challenges in the past and I've always landed on my feet."

Exercise: Answering Your "What If" Questions

If you find yourself in the habit of using rhetorical "what if" statements, here's a method for dealing with them:

1. Write down a "what if" question you've used.

   _____

   _____

   _____

2. If the way you've phrased the question is highly dramatic, change it to a less dramatic one. (Example: What if my headache means a brain tumor? Change it to: What if my headache doesn't go away?)

   _____

   _____

   _____

3. Now answer your "what if" question and see if the answer helps you become more decisive or clarifies what your next step will be.

_____

_____

_____

For example, Thomas, a sales supervisor, has put off making a commitment to a long-overdue vacation. "What if I can't get the time off?" he asks. "What if I make plans and we're at war again?" But he admits that his dramatic "what if" statements are ways of making himself feel important and irreplaceable at work. A war might mean "Let's not go overseas," but it shouldn't mean "Let's not go on vacation." His "what if" statements have functioned as a way to avoid making a decision.

When Thomas took the time to answer his "what-if" questions, he concluded that he could take a week's vacation during his company's slow season. He and his wife had saved enough money to take a trip, and they knew of several places they'd like to visit. Thomas says, "By coming to a decision, I made my wife very happy and felt satisfied myself. I enjoy vacations—I just get anxious with the planning stage."

In short, there's a big difference between asking questions that you don't even try to answer and answering the questions you raise in a helpful, resourceful manner.

Where Do You End Your Sentence?

Where you end your sentence makes a difference in how you feel now and in how you will feel in the future. Some endings can contribute to your feeling hopeless, incompetent, and overwhelmed. On the other hand, other endings can help you feel competent, effective, and empowered. Never let "I can't" or "I don't know" statements stand all on their own. Instead, change them to more empowering, less distressing sentences by adding a second, more upbeat thought so that your statement concludes with options and possibilities. Consider the following examples.

First, finish the following sentences with details relevant to your life.

- I can't _____

- I don't know how _____

Now enrich your sentence by adding, "but one thing I can do is" or "one thing I do know is" and complete the thought.

Jason, who's a Compliant person, is jittery about air travel. He tells himself, "I can't decide whether to visit my folks this year because I'm so nervous about flying." Making this categorical statement does nothing to help Jason come to a decision.

But notice what happens when Jason changes his sentence by adding the phrase "but one thing I can do is. . . ." "I can't decide whether to visit my folks this year because I'm so nervous about flying, but one thing I can do is to increase my phone calls and e-mails to them, or else take the train if need be." This way, Jason's statement ends with options and possibilities rather than with fear and indecisiveness. Can you see how adding that second clause gives him some breathing room? He's no longer trapped in what he doesn't know. Now he's thinking about alternatives, options, flexibility—an escape hatch from what would otherwise be a trap.

Marti, a Controlling person, falls into a similar trap. She intensifies her fear by telling herself, "I have to do so much for the holidays, and I don't know how I'll ever get it done." Not only does she start out with *I have to*; she also continues by saying *I don't know how*—a statement that leaves her feeling that she has no control over her situation. No wonder she's apprehensive! A revised statement immediately gives her some breathing room: "I want to do so much for the holidays and I don't know how I'll ever get it done, but one thing I do know is. . . ." She's no longer boxed into a corner. She's not responsible for everything. She can modify and amplify the statement based on more pragmatic information: ". . . but one thing I do know is that I'll have help decorating the tree. And I'll have dinner ready at some point. And it will be fine, even if it's not picture perfect."

This sort of simple, straightforward verbal addition can relax you, empower you, and even encourage a sense of humor about what previously seemed insurmountable problems and obstacles.

Here's another example: "I don't know how I'll ever get this task done on time, but one thing I *do* know is _____ ." Once again you have all sorts of options. The following are just a few alternatives that your thinking can take to finish the previous statement:

- "I don't know how I'll ever get this task done on time, but one thing I do know is I can ask my husband [or wife] to help me."

- "I don't know how I'll ever get this task done on time, but one thing I do know is I can let my boss know I need more time."

- "I don't know how I'll ever get this task done on time, but one thing I do know is I can get at least one part of the project finished by Friday."

Thoughtful Use of the Word But

"But" is such a little word. Yet it's power is pretty amazing. In a "but" sentence, one part is positive and hopeful, whereas the other part is negative and problematic. Always try to end your sentence with the more hopeful part coming *after* the "but." Here are two examples:

- "I'm not sure how to tell my daughter that I've been diagnosed with cancer, but I'll ask for my therapist's help with this situation."

- "It's awful that I lost half my retirement fund with the sagging economy, but I now know that I need to be more active in managing my money."

Even though these two situations are anxiety producing, you can see that they end with a plan for positive action.

Here's another example: Phil says, "I'm not sure if Tina will accept my proposal." The uncertainty of this situation is making Phil pretty skittish, so he has put off proposing to his girlfriend for over three months now. He just can't muster the courage to ask her to marry him.

Now watch the power of the word *but*. "I'm not sure if Tina will accept my proposal, *but* I know she loves me." The word *but* allows

Phil to deal not only with his fear ("I'm not sure if Tina will accept my proposal) but it also lets him feel hope ("I know she loves me").

To make this powerful word work for you, you must be aware of where you're using it. Since the most important part of your message comes after the *but*, make sure that this part is the more hopeful. For instance, if your boss says to you, "You're doing a good job, *but*" you anticipate that bad news will follow. Intuitively, you know the part before the but is just softening the blow. Contrast that statement with, "You're often late, but . . ." Intuitively you know that better news will follow the *but*, such as "You're often late, but you're doing a good job."

Exercise: Keep Track of Your But

I'd like you to write a few *but* sentences now. Put the first part of the sentence as something apprehensive; make the second part more encouraging or reassuring.

1. _____

but _____

2. _____

but _____

3. _____

but _____

Filter Out the Hurtful Part of the Criticism

One of the biggest fears that many people have (particularly people with the Compliant fear style) is fear of other people's criticism.

Perhaps you wish nobody ever criticized you at all, because you're sensitive, or you were raised to be "special," or you just don't like it. A world without criticism may seem to be ideal, but realistically speaking, you need feedback from other people, and sometimes that feedback will be hurtful. The good news, however, is that criticism can help you understand what you need to do to improve yourself. If you shut yourself off from criticism, you're practically begging for bigger problems, for minor irritations will almost invariably turn into major resentments.

Since being on the receiving end of criticism is a part of life, one of the greatest gifts you can give yourself is learning to hear the criticism without becoming defensive. Of course, it helps if the other person gives supportive and constructive criticism, but not all criticism is going to be constructive. For this reason, you need to learn to filter out the hurtful aspects of criticism while taking in the helpful aspects so that you can benefit from what you hear.

Destructive, harsh criticism typically involves these elements:

- A global, all-encompassing statement, such as: "You never do anything right," or "You always do this to me."

- Guilt-producing accusations, such as: "You don't care about anybody," or "Look at what you made me do."

- Impatience and coercion, such as: "I don't want to hear your excuses" or "If you loved me, you wouldn't do that."

If you can filter out the punitive, hurtful part of the criticism and not take it personally, your fears will diminish significantly. Rather than interpreting criticism as a massive assault on your personality, try to see it in more behavioral terms (e.g., "I didn't do this well," rather than "I'm an idiot.").

Consider these examples:

- When you hear someone say, "You never do anything right," change the words (in your head) to: "She's disappointed that I didn't do this right [or didn't do it her way]."

- When you hear someone say, "You always do this to me," say to yourself: "I did do it, but I didn't do it to hurt him deliberately."

Removing the Sting

Here are a few of my favorite phrases that can help you remove the sting of hurtful criticism: "Sometimes," "Right now," or "This time."

These phrases put criticism into a specific context of time. Even if the criticizer accuses with open-ended duration ("You *never* _____ [fill in the blank with a complaint]") you should translate the accusation to mean:

- "*Sometimes* I don't listen."
- "*Right now* I'm not paying attention."
- "*This time* I came across as too harsh."

These three phrases make the criticism time-limited, which helps you acknowledge that things can and will likely be different at another time.

So What?

"So what" is an antidote to believing that the criticism is something really, really bad. Initially, this phrase may seem to imply that you don't care. That's not what I intend. Rather, it puts criticism into a specific context of severity. If you can answer the question "so what?" many seemingly terrible or unpleasant experiences are likely to appear less drastic—not as calamities, but as problems to solve or as difficulties to manage or endure.

Criticism: "I don't think your son will be accepted at an Ivy League school."

Your response: "So what? He'll get into a college that's right for him. There are lots of good schools where he can obtain an excellent education."

Criticism: "Your presentation to the human resources department wasn't up to par."

Your response: "So what? This was the first time I spoke to this group. After I read the evaluations, I'll be able to improve my next presentation."

Criticism: "With skating skills like yours, you're likely to fall and break your ankle."

Your response: "So what? If I do, it won't be the end of the world. If that happens—which it probably won't—I'll deal with it."

Exercise: Take an Active Approach to Hearing Criticism

Now let's put into practice all the techniques I've described. Start by writing down some criticism that you've had to deal with:

_____

_____

_____

Consider these questions and comments:

1. What part of the criticism do you agree with?

2. What part do you disagree with? Example: "She thought I was rude, but I think she was provoking me."

3. What part is destructive and harsh? Change that to words that are less destructive, less harsh, but still true. Example: "I may have been insensitive but I'm not rude or thoughtless."

4. Now say the less destructive words, but either use "sometimes," "right now," or "this time." Examples: "Sometimes I'm so rushed that I forget how important it is to be sensitive," or, "Right now I'm under a lot of pressure, so I wasn't as sensitive as I should have been," or "This time I was insensitive."

5. Add "So what?" to the criticism. "When I get overwhelmed, I know I can become insensitive. So what? I know it would be best for me not to act this way, but I don't do it all the time, and I always apologize when I do."

Practice this sequence of steps with one or two other criticisms you've had to cope with. Congratulations! Your ability to deflect harsh criticism will have a direct effect on reducing your fears.

Appreciate the Value of Silence

In the attitude of silence the soul finds the path in a clearer light, and what is elusive and deceptive resolves itself into crystal clearness.

—MAHATMA GANDHI

Finally, here's my closing advice about the relationship between language and fear. Exaggerated words and self-defeating speech patterns aren't the only things that can intensify your fears. Too many words can also do this. At times we chatter away so much that we don't make time to be quiet, to give consideration to what really matters, to pay attention to our innermost feelings. An overabundance of words (what we say out loud as well as the buzz in our heads) can become noise. Like music without rests, what we experience is cacophony. Excessive talk can be the death of solitude and peace. When you silence the chatter, you give yourself an opportunity to listen to yourself, to hear what you think, and to acknowledge what you need to face.

9

Steps for Tuning In to Your Body

We are afraid because we run away; we don't run away because we are afraid.

—WILLIAM JAMES

KEITH HADN'T THOUGHT ABOUT HIS FATHER IN MANY YEARS. Then, on a day when he was feeling pretty low, Keith became overwhelmed by memories that distressed him both physically and emotionally.

What he recalled was an incident that had taken place when he was ten years old. His father had been pressuring him to jump off a five-foot diving board at the local pool. Keith remembered standing at the edge, looking into the water, and trying to muster the courage to take the plunge. He remembered trying, really trying, but he just couldn't do it.

"Let's go, boy!" his father yelled. "I don't have all day!"

Keith had felt stuck—unable to jump yet unable to turn around and get off the board.

"Just do it, Keith! Don't think, just do it! It's no big deal."

He had wished it *was* no big deal, but for him it was. He felt more and more terrified as he looked at the water, heard his father shouting, and saw the other kids staring. But he could only stand there, his limbs frozen, his heart pounding.

When the lifeguard finally rescued Keith from the diving board, his father launched into a tirade that seemed to go on forever. "What's the matter with you? You're ten years old, not two. It doesn't take any skill to jump off a low board like that. If you can't push past your fear and take action, you'll never amount to anything."

Now, decades later, Keith faced a totally different crisis, yet in his gut, his heart, his legs, and his whole body the situation felt the same. He had learned that a job promotion he'd been expecting had gone to someone else. That was bad enough. When he told his wife, though, Mandy surprised him by yelling, "I can't believe it! You'll never get a promotion if you don't speak up. You've got to be more aggressive or you'll never amount to anything."

Mandy's words hit him like a punch in the gut. In a split second he felt once again like that ten-year-old boy—humiliated, embarrassed, and paralyzed with fear. His heart pounded, his knees shook, and an icy chill went down his spine. Keith felt almost as helpless in responding to his wife's accusation as he'd felt many years earlier in responding to his father's.

What the Body Knows

It wasn't only Keith's brain that had stored the memory of that awful day on the diving board. That memory was also stored in his body, triggered anew when Mandy responded to him with anger. Although her words stung, Keith's bodily response was most influenced by the nonverbal cues: that sharp tone of voice, that menacing facial expression, that threatening finger pointing at him, insinuating how worthless he was.

You can feel fear in the body in many ways—from a general feeling of tension and tightness to headaches, shoulder pains, stomachaches, high blood pressure, a weakened immune system, impaired memory, and fatigue. Since these bodily responses happen below your radar of consciousness, you may not realize you're afraid until some time afterward. As Keith said in his therapy session, "I didn't think of myself as afraid until I recognized how my body responded. The only thing I was consciously aware of at the time was how ashamed I felt that I'd disappointed my wife." Fear as a physical response often precedes fear as a mental experience.

You may think your mind is the control center and knows everything that's going on inside you, but your body knows things that your mind isn't conscious of.

- Your senses may acquire information that your mind ignores.
- Your body may remember trauma that your conscious mind has forgotten.
- Your body may register fear that you aren't aware of yet.
- Your mind may deny fear, yet fear can still sap your energy and diminish your confidence.

The body refuses to be ignored. The body speaks its own language, and it doesn't mind telling you how it feels. You may feel fear in the body in many ways, which is richly described in our colloquial language.

- I'm losing control of my body.
- I'm sweating bullets.
- I can feel the hairs on my neck rising.
- My heart is pounding.
- I've got a knot in my stomach.
- I'm breaking out in a cold sweat.
- My skin is clammy.
- I'm shaking like a leaf.
- My legs feel like rubber.
- I'm so scared I'm frozen stiff.
- I've gone numb.
- My palms are soaked.
- I've got a lump in my throat.

Sometimes, but not always, these symptoms and sensations are a response to past trauma. Keith's humiliating boyhood experience on the diving board, for instance, has unquestionably contributed to his ongoing fear of confrontation. Similarly, if you were attacked by a dog during childhood, you may tense up at the sound of barking or at the approach of an unfamiliar pet. Crime victims often experience flash-backs when hearing, smelling, or seeing certain stimuli that remind them of their trauma. For months following the September 11 terror-ist attacks, many Americans experienced strong gut-level fear at the sound of airplanes overhead.

Many people think that the way out of fear is through controlling your thoughts—that thinking logically will ease the fears you feel in your body. Sometimes, this approach works. For instance, if you learn more about a medical procedure, you may feel better about it and calm down. But other times you can't logically make fear go away. Picture a person who is afraid of flying despite knowing all the sta-tistics about how "safe" flying is compared to driving. Yet, just the thought of flying puts her body into fear mode.

Therefore, to be able to fear less and live more, you need to learn a whole repertoire of new responses—using your mind, your voice, your behavior, and at times your body. Because each of these areas is part of a rich four-way interactive network (each one influences the others), you can begin your change process wherever you feel like beginning. In this chapter, the focus will be on the body—how it reg-isters and remembers fear—and what you can do to free your body from fear.

The Physiology of Fear

Let's consider briefly how fear works physiologically within the human body.

1. The amygdala, an almond-shaped mass of gray matter in the brain, is the body's fear command center—the first area of the brain to respond to stimuli that signal potentially threatening situations.

2. Neural activity in the amygdala triggers an unconscious (reflexive) fear response—a lifesaving response to danger that has evolved over time through evolution.

3. The thalamus routes information from the eyes and ears to areas of the brain for processing.

4. Stress hormones (epinephrine, norepinephrine, and cortisol) prompt the heart to pump harder, the lungs to work faster, and the brain to enter into a state of heightened alertness.

5. Other areas of the brain, such as the hippocampus, help to evaluate threats by placing them in context with earlier experiences.

6. Higher centers of the brain then spring into action. Your sensory cortex will assist you in separating an actual threat from a false alarm. Is that noise you hear behind you somebody stalking you, or is it just the wind? Your prefrontal cortex acts as the executive in charge, processing all the information you've received from the various parts of your body and brain and assesses whether the threat is indeed significant, and if so, what to do about it.

Stimuli that may put you at risk elicit two response systems in the brain. The first one is unconscious and automatic. It shoots from the hip, reacting without thinking. The second one is conscious and evaluative. It assesses the information to determine if the fear is warranted. If the fear is not warranted, it reins in the amygdala and your body returns to its normal state.

Let's see how you might experience these sequences in a real-life situation. Suppose you're walking in the woods. The corner of your eye catches something moving. Your amygdala responds. Automatically, you leap back as a self-protective response. You now take a closer look to see what the object is. Your sensory and prefrontal cortex help you assess the risk. If it's a squirrel running away from you, no problem; the fear is over in a flash. You continue on your way. If it's a snake, then your mind and body will formulate an emergency response.

In people with a fearful lifestyle, however, the prefrontal cortex may lose its ability to reign in the amygdala. The result is that fear is consistently aroused, even in nonthreatening situations. Because of the atmosphere in the world today, constant fear arousal is much more frequent than it has been previously. And I'm not just talking about terrorism and war.

A Formula for Fear

Here are excerpts from an e-mail I received recently, titled "Safety for Women."

> Something like 99% of us will be exposed to, or become a victim of, a violent crime. JUST A WARNING TO ALWAYS BE ALERT AND USE YOUR HEAD!!!
>
> If you are ever thrown into the trunk of a car, kick out the back tail lights and stick your arm out the hole and start waving like crazy.
>
> Always be aware. You MUST know where you are and what's going on around you.
>
> Wrong Place, Wrong Time. DON'T walk alone in an alley, or drive in a bad neighborhood at night.
>
> Don't just sit in your car after an activity. The predator will be watching you, and this is the perfect opportunity for him to get in the passenger side, put a gun to your head, and tell you where to go. AS SOON AS YOU GET INTO YOUR CAR, LOCK THE DOORS AND LEAVE.
>
> When you get into your car, be aware: look around you, look into your car. If you are parked next to a big van, enter your car from the passenger door. Most serial killers attack their victims by pulling them into their vans while the women are attempting to get into their cars.
>
> As women, we are always trying to be sympathetic: STOP IT! Sympathy may get you raped or killed. Ted Bundy, the serial killer, was a good-looking, well-educated man, who ALWAYS played on the sympathies of unsuspecting women. He walked with a cane, or a limp, and often asked "for help" into his vehicle or with his vehicle, which is when he abducted his next victim.
>
> Send this to any woman you know that may need to be reminded that the world we live in has a lot of crazies in it . . . better safe than sorry. IT IS ALWAYS BETTER TO BE SAFE THAN SORRY. (And better paranoid than dead.)

I'm flustered just reading this e-mail. Imagine if I took all its advice to heart, always reminding myself that I might be raped or killed on my way to the supermarket. Imagine constantly refreshing my memory that the world is full of crazies. This e-mail, if taken literally, is a formula for developing chronic fear: think about every situation as dangerous, every male sitting in a van as a potential kidnapper, and every handicapped guy as a potential serial killer. And just think, if I act on the suggestion to forward the e-mail to every woman I know, I can spread hysteria around the globe.

Now, I don't mean to say that some of those suggestions aren't good things to know. Of course it's good to be aware of your surroundings. That way you won't fall on your face, you'll cross the street safely, and you'll also see a friend you want to say hello to. Of course you should lock your car doors and not walk alone in a dark alley in a bad neighborhood. But these are safety precautions that you can take without the atmosphere of fear that this e-mail is hawking. I must admit that there was one helpful hint I'd never thought about before—what to do if somebody throws me into a trunk of a car. Okay, I'm prepared for that contingency now, so I can put it out of my head. But imagine how an overly reactive woman might respond to this. Can you picture her checking out the trunks of cars looking for a hand that's waving like crazy?

And can you imagine a susceptible child being raised by frenzied parents who keep warning their kid of the "dangers out there?" Is it any wonder that with such a communiqué, the amygdala hijacks the thinking part of the brain, leaving a person reacting to everyday situations as if they were life-threatening emergencies?

Recognizing Your Body Response Style

Just as we develop different styles of thinking and speaking about fear, we also develop habitual body response styles. Three styles that are typical among people who live in fear are hypersensitive, overreactive, and frozen.

Hypersensitive

Some people are physically and emotionally very sensitive. Aware of minute shifts and subtleties in how their bodies react, they find it burdensome to interact with the world. It's as if they have an allergy to life. Daily stresses and strains that bounce off others affect them intensely. It's as if they have no shock absorbers to protect them from life's jolts.

For as long as he can remember, people have been telling Edwin that he's too thin-skinned. His parents hoped that he'd somehow outgrow this sensitivity, but he never did. Today, at age thirty-eight, he's so overly reactive to what other people say that an offhand remark can throw him into a tailspin. His older brother, irritated by Edwin's hypersensitivity, calls him Bubble Boy and ridicules him by saying, "Get real! You act as though you have to live in a sterile, pain-free zone." It's true that Edwin has a comfort zone the size of a postage stamp. When he's outside that zone, he panics, pulls back from others, and stays trapped in a state of excessive self-absorption. To make matters worse, he is on high alert even when he's alone, predicting danger with every new body sensation. He feels lonely and scared, much like a young child who finds that his parents have gone out and he's left all by himself. His body responds as if there's a crisis at hand, even when nothing unusual is happening. Since he's been in therapy, Edwin is making an effort to redirect his attention to stimuli that calm him rather than stimuli that alarm him. Edwin hates his hypersensitivity. It's resulted in so much wasted time and so much wasted energy.

Overreactive

Other people are overly reactive in their response to fear. Because they can't tolerate tension in their body, they move quickly and impulsively to do something to feel better. They take action before they take the time to assess or evaluate a situation, letting their distressed feelings dictate their response. Because they react so impulsively, they have no time to choose a response from a repertoire of possibilities. Instead, they just leap headlong into situations and hope for the best.

Tammy exhibits this kind of behavior. Her inability to tolerate anxiety prompts her to take abrupt, often self-defeating actions—case in point: her recent move. Feeling lonely and isolated in a new city, she quickly responded when Larry, her boyfriend, who was also her boss, invited her to move in with him. Two months later, when Larry and Tammy broke up, she realized the costs of her impulsiveness: no apartment, no job. Tammy needs to learn how to become less reactive and more responsive. The difference is that reactive is reacting impulsively, without thought in an effort to get rid of the distress. (Is it any wonder that Tammy has no savings, since her favorite reaction is "shop till you drop"?) In contrast, responding is inner-directed. It requires a strong sense of self, which, despite the fear, lets you assess a variety of responses you could take before you act. It's no coincidence that the words *responding* and *responsibility* come from the same root.

Frozen

Still other people develop a rigid body style. Even when there's no imminent danger, their bodies are tight, stiff, and inflexible, as if they're on active duty in the military. Most people know about the common stress responses of fight or flight. The third type of response—seen a lot among animals—is to freeze: be still, don't respond, stay quiet, maintain camouflage, conceal, cover up, play dead. This is the habitual response system I call frozen.

Sal is a good example of the frozen response to fear. He is kinesthetically numb, deadened to feelings. He views his body as a machine, an entity separate from his self. It's a rare occasion when he shows any emotion. His girlfriend, Aletha, calls him a scarecrow and says that when she talks with him, it's like "talking to a brick wall." Sal responds to emotional situations in a mechanical manner, although Aletha is sure there must be feelings underneath. When she confronts Sal about being more emotional, he becomes even more rigid and hardened. "I just can't change," he says, and his tight facial features underscore his words.

Exercise: What's Your Body Response Style?

Read the following questions about the three body response styles, putting a check next to those that apply to you:

Hypersensitive

——— Do you think of yourself as having a sensitive body?

___ Are you aware of small shifts and subtleties in your body?

___ Do daily stresses and strains exhaust you?

___ When you're upset, does it take you longer than most people to get over it?

___ Does extraneous noise interfere with your concentration or relaxation?

___ Are you very sensitive to the temperature being too hot or too cold?

___ Are you very sensitive to what other people say?

___ Do you wish you had better "shock absorbers" built into your body, to help you deal with life's jolts?

Total number of checks ___

Overreactive

___ Do you hate to just "stay" with uncomfortable feelings?

___ Do you often plunge right into situations before you have a chance to think about your options?

___ Do you think of yourself as impulsive?

___ Are you a spontaneous, spur-of-the-moment person?

___ Have you taken hasty, rash actions that you later regretted?

___ Do you get restless when you need to stay still for any length of time?

___ Is your body always on the move, looking for action?

___ Is it difficult for you to calm your body down when you're excited?

Total number of checks ___

Frozen

___ Do you often keep your body rigid or still?

___ Do you think you're not as emotional as most other people?

—— Do you tend to tighten up when stressed?

—— Do you often keep your arms crossed and held tight against your body?

—— Do you clench your fists without even being aware of it?

—— Do you find it hard to relax your body even when you are on vacation?

—— Is it very important for you to be in control of your emotions?

—— Do you feel it's best to keep your feelings to yourself?

Total number of checks ____

Compare the number of check marks for each body response style. A greater number for one style indicates an inclination toward that style. It's possible for you to relate to more than one style because the boundaries between categories are porous, not rigid. Still, you probably will recognize that one of these is your customary style.

Since you've lived with your bodily response for such a long time, you may think there's nothing unusual about how you react to stimuli. When your fear level is quite high, you're certainly aware of it. But you may be aware that you hold a low level of fear in your body all the time, constantly feeling somewhat apprehensive. There's no one best response style, but too much of anything can create problems. The aim in dealing with this issue is to avoid the extremes—to keep your responses in moderation.

- If your habitual body response style is hypersensitive, give less attention to what's going on in your body; don't make what you feel in your body so important. Focus your attention outward on activities and images that do not stimulate your fear.

- If your habitual style is overreactive, see if you can tolerate having anxious feelings in your body without doing anything. Just stay with it. Take time to think before acting impulsively.

- If your habitual style is to freeze up when threatened, try to be more "loose as a goose." Flop, plop, and bop. Stretch, bend, and yield. Shake your booty, wiggle your hips, beat your feet.

Creating a Good Balance

Maintaining internal balance is necessary for the body to survive and to have a sense of well-being. This balancing process is called *homeostasis*. Much of it is managed by innate and automated physiological processes. Thus, you usually don't have to be concerned about regulating your body temperature or fighting off bacteria; your body does it for you. With other situations, all you have to do is follow your body's cues and you'll create a balance. This applies to the basic body functions of sleeping, eating, and eliminating.

Emotional problems, however, can throw off the homeostatic process. If you're depressed, you'll probably be sleeping or resting too much. If you're anorexic, you won't be eating enough. And if you are an "anal" personality, you most likely will be constipated, holding on to what you need to let go of.

Creating a balance in your life relates not only to the physiological processes, but also to how you respond to life's threats and challenges. If your need for safety is so strong, don't be surprised if you're living your life in fear. To change the pattern, you need to strive for a balance in which you're careful, but not too careful; vigilant, but not hypervigilant; aware, but not overly aware. In your work and personal goals, you need to seek accomplishment, not perfection; realism, not idealism. Aiming for attainable goals will diminish your fears; expecting the unattainable will increase your fears.

Exercise: Balance Is the Happy Medium

1 Take an 8½ × 11-inch sheet of paper.
2. Draw a vertical line down the middle. This line helps to illustrate dichotomous thinking (only two alternatives): good and bad, right and wrong, fearful and unafraid. We're all tempted to use this sort of thinking, but it has real limitations. You want to move from thinking dichotomously to thinking on a continuum.
3. Now take another sheet of paper and draw a horizontal line in the middle of the paper. This is what I call the continuum line.
4. Mark the number 1 at one end and the number 10 at the other end.

5. Write the numbers 2 through 9 evenly spaced along the line.

6. Here's what I'm getting at. Let's say you came from a house in which you had an overprotective parent (10 on the continuum). If this was your childhood experience, you may strive to be so different that you become an *under*protective parent (1 on the continuum).

7. Now look at the diagram you've created. At first glance, these two positions (1 and 10) look as if they're very distant from one another. Until . . .

8. You take the paper and bend it back as though you're making a cylinder out of it. You've turned a two-dimensional paper into a three-dimensional object.

9. What do you notice? The 10 is adjacent to the 1: When viewed this way, you can clearly see that the extremes, (the overprotective and underprotective parents) are more like each other than the parent who has taken a more middle-of-the-road approach.

10. What is furthest away? It's the 5—the balanced in-between position, that usually is indicative of a more composed, stable, self-assured person.

Listen to Your Body (but Not *Too* Much)

Learn to listen to your body.

- Let your body feel what it feels.
- Be aware of the sensory impressions that it's giving you.
- Oversee your body without micromanaging it.
- Do not attempt to change your sensations. Respect your body for its memories, desires, and needs.
- Listen to your body to discover what you're ready for.
- Protect your body from your bullying mind (if, for instance, you're torturing yourself with *have to*'s or *shoulds*).
- Don't try too hard. Gently encourage yourself, but don't push your body beyond its limits.

- Pay attention to your body's need for rest.
- Always keep breathing. (I kid you not—fearful people often hold their breath.)

Trial by Fire—Jeff's Story

Jeff, a well established furniture designer from Michigan, was preparing for his first speaking engagement at a trade show in New York City. Although he had spoken before at conferences and had received good feedback, his body was responding as though he was in a drastic, frantic situation. "This time it's different," Jeff said when he came to me for a consultation. "I'm so nervous that I'm contemplating reneging on my commitment, but I can't come up with a plausible excuse."

When I asked him why he had such an intense reaction to this particular speaking engagement, he replied, "This one will be in New York City. This is the major league. I'm afraid I'll make a fool of myself. I doubt if I can measure up to the quality of speakers who'll be at such a high-end show."

Soon I learned of a complicating factor. Precisely at a time when Jeff needed a little encouragement and kindness to face the challenge, his mind was reverting to his high school years, when "everybody thought of me as a dork." Almost twenty years had passed since that time, yet the body memory still had the power to undermine his confidence.

The more Jeff obsessed, the tighter his body became. He found himself in a typical approach-avoidance conflict: "I want to but I don't want to," he complained. "I'm excited to be doing this but I'm afraid it will be my Waterloo." Jeff's spirit was sinking fast.

He had come to me as his last hope to see if I could reduce his anxiety about this particular speaking engagement. Here's how I approached the situation.

First, I asked him to take three deep breaths and, on the third exhalation, to silently say something to himself that he found reassuring. Then I asked him what he'd said. His response: "I'll be okay; I'll get through this."

Then I asked him to remember a successful speaking engagement in the past. He recalled a time when he'd been not only knowledgeable but funny. The audience loved him and appreciated the slides he'd showed. I asked him how his body felt during this speaking engagement. He replied, "Relaxed and calm."

I set the stage in my office and created a makeshift podium. I asked Jeff to imagine the two hundred people that he expected would be attending his talk at the New York trade show. My intention was to do a type of make-believe exposure therapy. I asked him to imagine seeing a friendly face in the audience. I told him to smile at this person and nod a sign of recognition. Then I asked Jeff to remind himself why he was invited to speak at this conference. What was his expertise? Why did people want to hear what he had to say? Answering those questions got him to redirect his energy and attention outward, away from his body.

I then asked him to tell me what his opening sentence would be. He did, and it was a good one. As he continued speaking, I could feel him moving through the resistance. I could hear the change in his voice—more confident, less resistant. I could see his body unwinding, his facial muscles softening. I could see his breathing grow calm. In my office, at least, he had tamed his fear. I wished him well and bade him adieu. Two weeks later, when I received a thank-you note in the mail, I knew then that he had conquered his fear of speaking in the Big Apple.

What Jeff had learned is that, paradoxically, the body works better when you don't try too hard. Pushing your body when you're feeling tense and tight makes many tasks more difficult. By contrast, relaxing your body lowers your tension levels, making many tasks easier.

Try an Eastern Path

Meditation is the stilling of the thought-waves of the mind.

—PATANJALI

As members of a Western culture—and especially as Americans—our tendency is to respond to life in an outwardly energetic, even aggressive manner. Everything we do, we do (or think we should do) full blast. We work hard, play hard, exercise hard, even relax hard. We want to overcome every problem by sheer force of will. And when circumstances require backing off, waiting, or tolerating uncomfortable emotions instead of taking strenuous action, we often become irritated and impatient. In our culture, "giving in" to fear generally meets with disrespect, even contempt.

The Eastern way is different. It focuses more on cultivating the art of internal strength, which includes quiet, inner tranquillity, sitting still, and calming yourself rather than struggling against outward circumstances. Many Asians believe that doing a little is better than doing a lot, and doing nothing may even better. Doing nothing, however, does *not* mean entering into a weak, helpless state. You can do nothing yet be fully alive, fully aware. In Chinese medicine, for instance, the goal is to correct imbalances in our bodies so that blocked energy (*chi*) can flow freely again. In many yogic practices, developing resilience to adversity is more important than forcibly overcoming obstacles.

I doubt that Westerners can ever fully embrace the Eastern way of being, but we can certainly learn from Asian traditions. Yes, there are times when you should take action, but there are also times when taking action won't help, and what you need to do is simply let yourself *be*. You need to relax your nerves, your muscles, your mind, your body. The Asian wisdom traditions have much to offer in this regard.

User-Friendly Eastern Disciplines

Many people don't have any idea how to meditate, relax, sit still, or even take a nap. These nonactions may seem impossible to those who are entrenched in a fearful, busy, hectic lifestyle. But there are genuine virtues in these seemingly passive practices. Here are some Eastern disciplines that can help you cope with stress, tension, and fear:

- *Yoga.* Now widely integrated into American culture, yoga appears in many different forms throughout the country. Yoga practices include breathing, stretching, and relaxing the body and the mind, all in an effort to create an approach to life that is calm and peaceful.

- *Meditation.* Here again, what once seemed exotic has now become mainstream. Meditation emphasizes counting your breaths, monitoring the ebb and flow of thoughts within your mind, focusing on a concept, or repeating a mantra (a word or phrase that relaxes or concentrates the mind).

- *T'ai chi.* This ancient Chinese discipline—a form of martial arts modified to become meditation-in-motion—is accessible to people of all ages. Graceful in appearance, T'ai chi allows practitioners to "focus on the moment" through a sequence of motions that screens extraneous thoughts in the mind and relieves tension in the body.

- *Tae Kwan Do and other martial arts.* No longer limited to the young and belligerent, martial arts can be an avenue to renewed confidence, self-discipline, and inner calm. These disciplines are extremely varied in nature. Although often strenuous, they stress self-mastery and mindfulness more than outward manifestations, such as cracking boards or defeating opponents.

- *Qigong.* This Chinese discipline emphasizes reduction of stress and anxiety, improving overall physical fitness and flexibility, and quieting the mind. Qigong (pronounced "chi gung" or "chi kung") is a health system that stimulates the Qi (chi) or vital energy within the body through gentle movements, sounds, breathing, and meditation techniques.

Reduce Your Overload

You turn on the TV and hear about the latest terrorist threats, fatal car accidents, health hazards, and murder that has taken place in or close to your community. You can feel your body tensing up as you listen to the talking heads scaring you. But then you figure you've had enough. You turn off the TV. So why do you still have a knot in your stomach? Why do you feel a headache coming on?

The answer is that your body isn't a machine. You can't turn your engine off with a simple turn of the key, as you do with your car.

Feelings in your body can linger for a long time—even after the original stimulus is no longer present. Letting go of your nervousness isn't easy. Your body is designed to get revved up much more quickly than it's designed to calm down. And it could be that you never truly *do* calm down. You just maintain a lower level of chronic fear in your body. Over time, this may seem normal to you, but it isn't.

Kelly's Story

Kelly walked into my office visibly stressed. "I don't know how much more I can take," she complained. "This week was the worst! On top of a high terrorist alert, my son comes home with a progress note, my daughter has the flu, and my husband tells me that a client is suing him. It's too much for me to cope with! I am so afraid. I'm trying to keep sane, but there's so much worry in the pit of my stomach. I don't know what to do."

I told Kelly the first thing she needed to do was to relax. Nothing that she mentioned needed to be attended to right away. The house wasn't on fire, her daughter didn't need to be rushed to the hospital, her husband had hired an attorney to help him with his problem, no bombs were falling. Right now Kelly needed to focus on Kelly.

Before we tackled any relaxation exercises, though, I gave Kelly two guidelines to follow. First, I wanted her to set limits on fear-inducing stimuli. World events were beyond her control. Kelly's sensitive nervous system had enough stress from her personal life; she didn't need to get constantly worked up over calamities across the globe as well. I wasn't suggesting ignorance—just limiting stressful input. I told her to avoid TV news, Internet headlines, and the newspaper's front-page horror stories. She thanked me for giving her permission to avoid reading or watching the news.

Second, I wanted Kelly to avoid alarming conversations. Kelly had two friends whom she called "gloom-and-doom buddies." "We feed off of one another," she admitted, "each of us saying, 'Did you hear about this?' And then we discuss the latest health scare, car crash, or homicide." Those dreary discussions were taking a toll, so I told Kelly to change the topic to something more upbeat. If her buddies wouldn't cooperate, then I told her to limit her contact with them. Kelly readily agreed, for she knew that hysteria is contagious. She didn't want to contribute to it or be a victim of it.

Now it was time for Kelly to learn how to calm her body. She had spoken to her friend Nancy about yoga. She didn't know much about it, but heard it was great for relaxing and bringing peace of mind. "If there's anything I need, that's it," said Kelly, "but I don't know how I'll ever find time for it. It'll just be another task I have to do." Kelly's friend Nancy understood, but continued to encourage Kelly to join her. One day, much to Nancy's surprise, Kelly agreed. "I'll try it," she said without much enthusiasm, "but I don't know that I'll continue with it." Nancy replied, "No problem."

It took Kelly just one session to believe that yoga might be a better way of helping her relax than popping another Xanax. Her teacher, Jen, was so accepting that Jen's attitude astounded her in its own right. Brought up in a family with constant pressure to work harder, faster, better, Kelly had tears in her eyes when her teacher spoke calmly, saying, "It's okay—work at your body's own pace. Treat your body gently and lovingly."

Once Kelly was hooked on yoga's mental and physical benefits, she somehow found the time to get to class, always emerging with more energy and more acceptance—of herself and of "what is."

Circuit Breakers—A Good Thing

Before I end this chapter, I want to share with you a concept that has been helpful to many of my patients. I like to make an analogy between an overloaded body and an overloaded electrical system. Imagine that in your home office you have your air conditioner, your computer, your fax machine, your printer, your scanner, your TV, your radio, your clock, plus your overhead and task lighting all on one circuit. You remember that the guy who installed your computer suggested you put the computer and the air conditioner on their own circuits and you said you would—someday. But so far, you've had no problem. You usually get away with this overload because not all your machinery operates simultaneously.

Now, on this very day that you are operating on a tight deadline, the circuit breaker pops. Now nothing is working. It's dark, you're tense, and of all things you have to go search around for a flashlight. Finally you find it. Lucky you, the batteries are actually working! You locate the electrical panel, open it up, and search for the switch that was thrown. You flip it back on again and return to work, wondering how much data you've lost. You're just getting settled in when pop, you're in darkness again. You forgot to turn off some of the appliances before you got back to work. You hate this circuit breaker, thinking it's nothing more than a nuisance to you.

But then you remember: A circuit breaker is a safety device designed to prevent a fire that would probably occur if the overloaded condition continued for any length of time.

Do you see the analogy to your own life? If you're living a harried, pressured life, you most likely have an overloaded circuit yourself. If you didn't have so much to attend to, you wouldn't be so stressed about that last phone call. If you weren't so stressed, you wouldn't be so nervous about that upcoming event. If you weren't so nervous, you wouldn't be so irritable with your partner's lack of consideration. If you weren't so irritable with your partner, you wouldn't have this pounding headache. You get the picture?

Too bad we don't have a circuit breaker built in to our systems! Or do we? For what else is a nervous breakdown except a way that your system is telling you, "You can't live like this anymore"? What else is chronic stress, chronic fear, chronic irritability telling you except that something's got to change.

10

Steps for Being Footloose and Fear-Free

Breathing is so simple and so obvious that we often take it for granted, ignoring the power it has to affect body, mind, and spirit. Breathing can make us excited or calm, tense or relaxed.

—HARRIET RUSSELL

TO REDUCE THE BODY'S RESPONSE TO FEAR, the core issue is learning to relax. Your impression of relaxing may be popping a pill, grabbing a drink, smoking pot, reaching orgasm, zoning out, or becoming a couch potato. These ways have their place, but they don't relax the muscle system or the nervous system, not to mention their addicting potential or their problematic aftereffects.

Breathing and Muscle Relaxation

What follows are suggestions for how to relax and release energy that may be dormant or blocked as a consequence of tension. (Note that these suggestions may seem different from one another, even opposite in approach, yet they can still be effective.)

Slow, Deep Breathing

Slow, deep breathing and muscle-relaxing techniques are among the best and easiest ways to reduce fear in the body. Many people are aware of this, but they either don't know how to do them or think they are boring. For these reasons, I teach skills that add some unique aspects to relaxation techniques so that they are experienced as fun, interesting, or even silly. (It's hard to be silly and fearful at the same time.)

BREATH AWARENESS

Some people are so busy that they literally have to pause to catch their breath. They may be unaware that they're breathing shallowly, unevenly, or holding their breath. What is your breathing like right now? Is it quick or slow? Is it smooth or strained? Are you breathing from the chest or from your belly? Just becoming aware of your breath can start to calm you.

Read the next three sentences, then gently close your eyes and take three deep breaths, one after the other. Inhale s-l-o-w-l-y through your nose, then exhale s-l-o-w-l-y through your mouth. If you tend to exhale quickly, imagine that you're blowing on a spoonful of hot soup. As you do so, say (silently) something reassuring, such as, "I can handle it," or "It will be okay," and then repeat. This is one of the easiest, most effective exercises for calming yourself. When I do this with my patients, some of them relax so quickly and deeply that they start to yawn. Then at once they apologize, as if they've done something wrong. I tell them, "Don't apologize! I take it as a compliment. You arrived at my office upset, aggravated, and frustrated—and now you're relaxed enough to yawn." I don't take yawning as a social faux pas or a sign of boredom; to me, it means that my patients have let go of tension and are breathing smoothly and steadily. They're no longer tight and tense. I view that as a success because slow, deep breathing lowers the heart rate and quiets the mind.

INSPIREZ, SOUFFLEZ

I often teach my clients slow breathing with an exotic twist. I began to use this exercise after I took an Air France flight. The flight's video program included breathing, stretching, and relaxation exercises for passengers sitting in their seats. Americans tend to think that anything that comes from another country is exotic and intriguing. The French language added a touch of spice to what might otherwise have seemed mundane. Inhale, exhale (which sounds almost medical) was transformed into *inspirez, soufflez.*

The result? Now my clients weren't just inhaling. With every breath they were picturing themselves being filled with inspiration, life, and spirit. And they weren't just exhaling—they were letting excess air leave a puffed-up soufflé. All the healthy, sustaining nourishment was traveling to each and every cell of their bodies while all the toxins were exiting their bodies. *Inspirez-soufflez* may inspire better than inhale-exhale.

Tighten Up to Relax

How many times have people told you "Relax," "Take it easy," "Don't be so uptight?" But it's not so easy just to let go of the tension and tightness. Paradoxically, however, tightening up can help you relax, because when you exaggerate the tightness in your muscles it is easier to let go.

Here are two exercises I use with my patients.

TENSING YOUR ARMS

1. Clenching your fist, raise one of your arms up in the air.
2. Keeping your elbow bent, move your arm back to get leverage to land a blow.
3. Hold your arm and fist in that position.
4. Now, rather than bringing your fist all the way down, abruptly stop the movement midway.
5. Keep your arm in this midair position to a count of twenty. What do you feel? Do you feel incredible tightness, tension, even pain?
6. Go ahead and lower your arm whenever you feel you need to.

Keep in mind that the tension you've felt in this exercise is how some people hold fear and tension in their body all the time: with muscles constricted, circulation impeded, and tension all balled up in a knot. Once you learn to feel this tension clearly, it will be easier for you to take steps to relax and let go.

Progressive Relaxation

Here's a different exercise that takes that same sequence—increased tension leading to awareness—culminating in tranquillity. (Note: until you learn the sequence of steps from memory, record these instructions on a tape recorder to play back during the exercise, or have someone else read you the instructions while you follow them.)

1. Select a flat surface where you can lie comfortably. A bed is good, but a clean floor is preferable. Use a rug, blanket, exercise mat, or yoga mat if that makes you more comfortable.

2. Lying flat on your back, rest a few minutes, breathing slow, deep breaths and letting go of any worries of the day.

3. Starting with your right leg, raise your limb slightly off the floor.

4. Tighten, tighten, tighten the leg muscles.

5. Now relax, letting the leg drop back to a resting position. You'll find that following the initial surge of tension and release, the foot, calf, and thigh muscles will now feel calmer and less tense.

6. Proceed to the left leg, tightening all the muscles, letting the tension build, and then releasing the tension after a few moments.

7. Let the leg and the rest of your body relax for a few moments.

8. Raising your right arm a few inches off the mat right next to your body, tighten the fist, tighten the forearm, and tighten the upper arm as hard as possible.

9. Hold the tension, let it accumulate, and then release your arm, letting it drop to a resting position.

10. Repeat this sequence with your left arm, allowing the tension to build, hold, and release.

11. Now tighten your buttock muscles, which will raise your lower abdomen slightly, and let the tension accumulate.

12. Release. Bask in the calm that follows when you relax.

13. Move on to your abdomen: tighten the stomach muscles, hold the tension, and release.

14. Once again lie quietly for a few moments afterward.

15. Bending your arms at the elbows and pulling the elbows tightly against your sides, flex your biceps and tighten your chest muscles (pectorals) as hard as you can. Hold the tension, then release.

16. Rest quietly once again.

17. Raise your shoulders slightly off the floor and pull them toward each other, as if to make them touch, and tighten them hard until, as the tension builds, you feel a great urge to release. Release and relax.

18. Next, scrunch up your face—pucker your lips, squeeze your eyes shut, and tighten your cheeks—until the tension gets really tight.

19. Rather than releasing the tension immediately, though, first open your mouth wide, thrust your tongue out and down, and open your eyes as wide as possible. (Don't worry about how you look—no one is judging you.)

20. Now relax.

By completing this sequence, you've alternately stretched and relaxed almost every muscle in your entire body. Performing this exercise regularly, especially if you do it on a daily basis, can do wonders to shake off bodily stress and strain.

Reduce Fear Incrementally

Fear is an inevitable part of life, and sometimes it serves good purposes. Although it may be a beautiful fantasy to think of eliminating fear altogether, that wouldn't be feasible even if it were desirable. The same holds true for eliminating tension. A more realistic goal: reduce fear and tension to some degree. Bring it down a couple of notches. Assuming a one-to-ten scale, wouldn't you feel pleased simply to lower your fear and tension from, say, a level 10 to a level 7? Or from level 7 to level 4? Wouldn't it be better to feel concerned about a situation rather than acutely apprehensive?

Doing so may require some mind work. That's fine, since the mind and body are connected and mutually influential. The following is an example.

Jane was just a few hours away from a first date with Ben, a man who Jane's brother felt was a perfect match for her. As the get-together loomed, she felt acutely nervous, then almost panicky. "This is no way to begin a date," she said. "Why am I so nervous? Does it mean I'm scared to meet this guy—that I don't really want to? Or does it mean that I want to, but I can't contain my excitement?" Jane was onto something when she mentioned being scared in one sentence and excitement in the next. There's a fine line between fear and excitement, with the physiological responses being quite similar. For this reason, I suggested to Jane that she shift her thinking from fear to excitement. She agreed and admitted that she was very excited about the possibility that "today could be the day I meet 'the one.'" When she understood that her frenzy of excitement might be causing the butterflies in her stomach, her joy level shot up while her fear level plummeted.

If fear, worry, and anxiety are familiar ways of living to you, don't imagine that you'll suddenly wake up and find yourself laid back, at ease, and cool as a cucumber. It's not your nature. However, you can change little by little. And you have no choice but to start where you are, not where you'd like to be.

Here are some ideas to help you decrease your fear incrementally.

First, think about your fear level on a scale of 1 to 10. If your fear level usually rates a 10, your aim is to reduce it a few notches. The catch is to avoid getting too ambitious too soon. Steer clear of unrealistic goals. Accept where you are and accept the pace of your change. Tell yourself "It's okay," "I'm okay," or "The way I am is okay." If you aim too high (such as by expecting to leap from a 10 to a 2), you're setting yourself up for failure. A better strategy: aim to reduce your fear incrementally.

Second, surrender control. You don't have to *control* your fear; you can experience it, observe it, look at it, speak about it, or draw a picture of it. You can talk to your fear, be mindful of it, even appreciate it. But you don't need to control it. Trust that when you're ready to let go of it, you will. And you'll do so incrementally. Unless a kid is a real natural (and I don't know any kids like that), he doesn't take off his training wheels the first day he hops on a two-wheeler. Only when he trusts himself can he go riding off with abandon. And usually that success comes as a big surprise. He isn't even aware of how skilled he's become until one day he just does it. This will be true for you as well.

Third, respect your resistance. One part of you may say, "I'm sick and tired of living my life in fear. I'm ready to move on. I'm *more* than ready." That sounds great—you're highly motivated and ready to roll. However, don't be surprised if another part of you isn't quite ready to let go of your fears. This resistance is there for a reason. Don't try to ram through it. Don't force yourself to go beyond your readiness. Respecting your resistance may seem to slow you down, but it will be advantageous to you in the long run.

Mary, a Shy young woman, was nervous about speaking to her teacher regarding an English Lit grade that she thought was unfair. Her father taunted her about her resistance: "What's the big deal? The professor isn't going to bite you, so why are you so timid? Just do it!" Luckily, Mary didn't approach her teacher that day. She was feeling too bad about herself to do it. Instead of revving up her energy for action, her father's lecture had revved up her fear. The next few days, she kept clear of her intense father. She gave herself time to get past her resistance, gain her confidence, and think about how she wanted to speak to her professor. The following Wednesday, she felt ready. She was more composed; she'd planned what to say to the teacher; and although she felt a little nervous, she was not *too* nervous. She pleaded her case well. Although she could not convince her professor to change her grade, she felt satisfied with herself that she'd accomplished what she had set out to do.

Learn to Be Still

I have discovered that all human misfortune comes from this: the human inability to sit still in a room.

—Blaise Pascal

I hear so many stories from people these days talking about how crazy their lives are. They usually follow this complaint with a description about how they've been frantically running here, running there, taking care of this, that, and everything else. What's most amazing to me is that I hear this same complaint from everyone—from working women, full-time moms, men, kids, even retirees. Everyone's dashing about trying to do as much as they possibly can. Why are people always so busy? I can't answer that question (although I've got a few hypotheses), but I can tell you that constantly being on the go takes a toll. There's a big difference between being busy and being so busy that you can't find a moment to be still. If you spend your days dashing around, yet at the end of the day you feel that you haven't done enough, it's time to make a change. If your mind is racing as fast as your body, and your thoughts have proceeded to the next activity before you finish this one, it's time to make a change. This rush-around state creates great stress on mind and body alike. It's no wonder that so many people feel exhausted, tense, and anxious.

If this frenetic lifestyle sounds familiar, here's my advice. Each day create time for yourself to be still. Be silent. Seek solitude. Do nothing. It won't be easy, and being still may seem like a waste of time. After all, you've got so much to do! There's no time these days for rest or reflection or a quieter rhythm. The maze of daily responsibilities seems to gobble up all your choices. And what is lost? Or should I say, *who* is lost?

Once you get past the resistance to being still, however, that stretch of time can become the loveliest part of your day. Being centered, being in the moment, can bring about a deep sense of well-being. Stay still long enough and you'll begin to know yourself in a new way. How amazing it is to become really clear about what you feel, what you think, what you want, and what you value. And what a complete surprise it can be when this new stillness also eases your physical tension and calms your fears.

Try to imagine how your life might be different if each day you could:

- Have a place where you can simply *be*
- Listen to your own feelings
- Inhale the good air

- Let go of the tension
- Gently close your eyes
- Release the blockage
- Soften your body
- Relish the stillness
- Empty your data storage bank
- Let your mind drift to a pleasing state
- Feel what's deep within you
- Appreciate your solitude
- Connect with yourself
- Be your soul's best friend

Combine Body Movements with Incompatible Thoughts

Telling someone not to be afraid when he or she is afraid is often counterproductive. It just doesn't work. Trying to explain away the fear intellectually also has only a moderate chance of success. One method that does have a good success rate, however, is combining body movements with incompatible thoughts.

EXERCISE #1

S-T-R-E-T-C-H your arms way up to the ceiling. Now jump up and down like an excited kid and yell, "I'm afraid! I'm afraid! I'm afraid!" Can you stay fearful? The typical result of this exercise is laughter, since everyone instantly recognizes that an upbeat body doesn't have downbeat thoughts. In short, physical actions can overcome fear—even short-circuit it.

Another implication of this exercise: getting more physical activity can help you counteract fear. What works for me is going for a brisk walk, doing yoga, playing tennis, or dancing.

What physical activities do you think will help you short-circuit your fear?

_____

_____

_____

EXERCISE 2

Let your head and shoulders droop. Now imagine that you weigh a hundred pounds more than you really do, and that a huge burden of weight is bearing down on your shoulders. Now shout, "I'm so happy, I'm so happy!" Just as when you did the previous exercise (which is the mirror image of this one), you can't force yourself to feel what your body isn't feeling; once again, your body tells a message that's louder and clearer than what your words can say.

EXERCISE 3

Think of phrases you say that are typically associated with fear or frustration. Then think of an incompatible bodily action. Do this action. What are the results?

For Larry, the words were, "I can't take it anymore." When Larry felt like he'd had enough, he would typically go straight to the liquor cabinet or his stash of pot, believing that this was the only way he could mellow out. When I asked Larry to change this response, he balked. Still, I pushed him. His final answer: he started singing. No, *bellowing* would be a better word: "I gotta be me, I gotta be me! No matter what happens, I've gotta be me!" And all the while Larry was making vigorous arm gestures as accompaniment.

Now it's your turn. See what incompatible action you can associate with a fear thought.

Fear thought _____

Incompatible action _____

Fear thought _____

Incompatible action _____

Fear thought _____

Incompatible action _____

Seek Child's Play for Adults

The supreme accomplishment is to blur the line between work and play.

—ARNOLD TOYNBEE

Kids let loose so willingly. They release their energy, play, jump, run, skip, dance, roughhouse, leap, and roll around. They trust their bodies. They're naturally playful. They delight in rhythm, in making up songs, in finding ways to be silly. Children feel free to suspend control. But as adults, we find this difficult. We want to be in control.

Wouldn't it be great if you could let the "child" within you emerge (at times) and run free? Wouldn't it be wonderful if you could be spontaneous and let go of the urge to stay in control all the time? Wouldn't it be sensational to be adventurous instead of endlessly responsible? By all means be an adult, but let your inner kid have a little time in the sun, too.

Ask yourself these three questions:

- What helps you play?

- What helps you be free?

- What helps you be adventuresome?

Do you remember your favorite game as a child? For many people, it was some version of tag, jump rope, ball playing, catch, Frisbee—some form of letting loose, of delighting in motion, of enjoying the sheer pleasure of existence. Could you do something like that now? Of course many adults enjoy sports, and that's fine. But sports often tend to be organized and competitive. Despite all their delights, sports are *controlled*. How about letting loose in a more spontaneous, less controlled fashion? It may help you if there's a child or a pet in your family to play with; it's no surprise that kids and pets make us feel younger. But even without a willing accomplice of this sort, see what game you can play. If you're looking for an activity you can do by yourself, try skipping, bouncing a ball, singing a childhood song, swirling a hula hoop, or dancing.

Children are experts at having fun, letting loose, and being silly. At least now and then, let's emulate them.

Use Music to Change Your Mood

Music is well said to be the speech of angels.

—THOMAS CARLYLE

The consolations of music have age-old roots in most cultures, both in religious and secular settings. Many people find solace in singing hymns, songs, and even tunes they've made up themselves, or find comfort by listening to popular or classical music. During the months following the September 11 attacks, I noticed many people returning to patriotic songs that they hadn't sung in years, often without conscious awareness. "God Bless America" has been many people's favorite.

This hymn (as well as others, such as "America," "The Battle Hymn of the Republic," and "The Star-Spangled Banner") offers deep solace, warding off fear during dark times. The melody as well as the lyrics resonate with our collective unconscious, bringing us together as a community in our time of need. In this way music, particularly certain songs, can be a very therapeutic medium. Reassuring us like a caring parent, music calms the body and soothes the soul. Why? Because music bypasses the intellectual part of the brain and moves straight to the center of our being.

When you feel tense and fearful, I recommend that you let a song come to mind. Don't force it—just let a melody pop into your head. Some favorites include religious songs, which may have deep roots in your personal experience. Other people prefer patriotic songs or classic American folk songs. One African American friend calms herself by singing "We Shall Overcome," which holds great personal as well as ethnic significance for her. My son Brian finds his wide range of musical interests—from Springsteen to Stravinsky—a source of encouragement, and inspiration.

To find comfort in these and other kinds of music, you don't need to know all the lyrics or even the title. Sometimes it's the words that will do it for you; at other times it's the beat or the melody. Sometimes there's a line from a song that is so repetitive that it serves as a mantra. Many of Bob Marley's songs fit the bill—with phrases such as "Don't worry," "Be happy," "Everything's going to be all right"— repeated so many times that by the end of the song, you've absorbed his message. Whatever moves you, trust the unconscious process. Just as a dream can never be wrong, the music that touches your heart and soul can never be wrong.

Trust Your Intuition

Intuition isn't the enemy, but the ally, of reason.

—JOHN KORD LAGEMANN

One of the things I've noticed in my clinical work is that some people (men and women alike) are highly intuitive, while others don't seem to know intuition exists. What is intuition and why is it important? Intuition is knowledge that's gained without the direct use of rational processes. It's an impression, a perception, an insight whose origins you don't fully understand. It's located more in your body than in your conscious mind. It's what you feel in your gut or when something just doesn't feel right. If your intuition is good, it's an important source of information that can inform you when it's appropriate to feel afraid and when it's not. On one occasion it may save your life; on another occasion it may save you from worrying about danger that's actually minimal.

Those who do not trust their intuition—or even acknowledge that it exists—have one less source of information for good decision making. I'm not suggesting that intuition is error-proof or that it should replace rational thought processes, but I *am* suggesting that it's foolish to ignore what your body knows intuitively.

Listening to your intuition sometimes means paying attention to fear that you might otherwise ignore. Countless people have saved themselves from harm by trusting hunches they couldn't explain.

Many years ago, Vicki went camping with her teenage daughters in a region of the Rocky Mountains near the Big Thompson River in Colorado. A violent rainstorm started up during the night. Vicki had never seen such intense rain, and she grew more and more fearful about her own safety and that of Jenny and Laura. As the weather conditions deteriorated and runoff soaked the family's tent, Vicki was tempted to abandon the campsite and drive home to Denver. Yet a deep, gut-level hunch prompted her to stay put. She couldn't pick up any radio reports about the storm—broadcasts seemed to have been disrupted—but she worried that the rain might be creating even greater hazards elsewhere. Despite her daughters' pleas to leave, Vicki insisted on holding their ground. The three of them huddled in their car throughout a miserable night. Even the next day the torrential rainfall continued. Vicki and her daughters returned to Denver almost thirty-six hours later, taking a roundabout route home. They learned en route that the Big Thompson River had flooded so severely that almost a hundred people had died in the canyon, many of them campers attempting to flee the storm. Vicki's intuition had paid off. When asked why she felt that staying put was the right decision, she shrugged and said, "It just felt right."

I don't want to confuse intuition with impulsiveness. Impulsiveness is simply rushing through something to get it over with. Intuition, on the other hand, is based on impressions, premonitions, and other notions that are usually valid. With intuition, you don't always know why you know something; you just know that you know it. Perhaps we have some sense that hasn't been discovered yet. Perhaps we have some physiological abilities in common with animals, who know much of what they know without formal reasoning. (Among mammals there appear to be some with remarkable knowledge that defies explanation; I once read about a dog whose barking alerted a woman that her baby had stopped breathing—the dog knew intuitively that something was wrong.) Respect your intuition. It can give you important information that may lead to better decisions.

EXERCISE: GET IN TOUCH WITH YOUR INTUITION

Precisely because intuition is nonrational, it's often hard to pin down. But by doing a sentence-completion exercise, you may get a better sense of what your intuition is trying to tell you.

First, think about a situation that creates some fear in you. Then complete these sentences:

1. Despite my fear, one good thing about this situation is

   _____

2. In addition to my fear, I also feel _____

3. My fear is concealing _____

4. When I'm afraid, I have a tendency to ignore _____

5. When I'm more relaxed about this, I'll probably think

   _____

6. My sixth sense tells me that _____

7. I don't know but I have a hunch that _____

8. It may not make sense, but my gut instinct is telling me

   _____

You have to leave the city of your comfort and go into the wilderness of your intuition. What you'll discover will be wonderful. What you'll discover will be yourself.

—ALAN ALDA

Freeing Your Body, Freeing Your Actions

Throughout this chapter, I've suggested that by calming your body, you can mitigate your fears as well as free your mind and spirit.

What's just as important, however, is this: feeling less fear can lead in turn to greater freedom of action. And that's the subject we'll approach next.

11

Steps for Acting Your Way Out of Fear

You must do the thing you think you cannot do.

—Eleanor Roosevelt

WHAT'S ONE ACTION YOU WISH you could take right now and would do so if you weren't so afraid of doing it?

Would you ask your boss for a raise?

Would you contact a long-lost friend?

Would you travel to a place you've always wanted to visit?

Would you confront your parents about past misunderstandings?

Would you ask someone out on a date?

Would you take up a new sport?

If you can overcome your fears and reach out to the world, countless exciting, delightful, fulfilling experiences await you. But how can you do this?

One of the last strongholds for fearful people to overcome is to take action—not just to think or talk about overcoming fear, but to push past the fear and actually *do* new things. If you've been putting into practice some of the steps I've suggested in previous chapters, you know how much difference they can make. Now it's time to direct your attention toward acting your way out of fear.

Some people believe that they're unable to take action until some hypothetical moment in the future when they can set aside their fear once and for all. Others feel that they must hit rock bottom before they become motivated to change. Still others believe that change to a more action-oriented stance is possible, but it must happen totally— a complete transformation—or not at all. I disagree with these extreme views. I believe that change is always possible, and that it can take place gradually, even erratically, and still have immense value. Taking action doesn't mean you no longer feel any fear; it just means that you step past the fear and take action anyway. You can take action even when doing so is tough or terrifying. Far from being opposites, fear and action are a necessary and workable partner-ship—a partnership in which your skills increase, your experiences broaden, and your inner strength becomes more substantial.

In the face of fear, action is the most important definition of success in this change program. The ability to take action *despite* fear defines courage, denotes growth, and in the long run, sends fear packing. Imagine opening your life more often (and more fully) to new experiences. Imagine using your energy to act your way out of fear instead of wasting or constricting your energy so that nothing ever changes. In this chapter, I'll offer strategies that will help you make these goals a reality.

Strengthen Your Self Muscle

Knowledge must come through action.

—SOPHOCLES

We all understand the importance of physical exercise (even if we don't do it!). A growing body of evidence suggests that vigorous activity contributes to long-term fitness, agility, stamina, and overall well-being from youth well into old age. If, despite all this evidence, you still insist upon sitting on your duff day after day, your muscles will weaken, your body will become flabby, and you'll become increasingly out of shape.

A similar analogy relates to the self-muscle concept that I learned from my husband, health psychologist Ronald Goodrich. In order to strengthen the "self muscle," you need to take actions that work out your self-esteem, self-confidence, and self-respect. Perhaps you wish you could have a stronger sense of self or have more trust in your ability to deal with the challenges you face. Perhaps you wish you were more confident in handling your social or professional obligations. Perhaps you want to feel more secure in your parenting skills. Many aspects of your background—temperament, family experiences, and personal history, among others—influence your confidence in these matters. But whatever your past experiences, you can strengthen your self muscle by exercising it. Just as you can increase your physical power, stamina, and flexibility by working out, you can increase your emotional power, stamina, and flexibility by exercising your psychological "muscles."

By taking action, you can:

- Enhance your confidence.
- Accomplish tasks you've avoided.
- Succeed in areas in which you've failed.
- Complete jobs you've neglected to finish.
- Become more imaginative in your thinking.
- Become bolder in your response to challenges.
- Become more courageous in your dealings with the world.
- Feel good, and more important, feel good about yourself.

How? By doing the emotional equivalent of working out—that is, by exerting yourself, tackling progressively harder tasks, and building your confidence step by step.

Surprise Yourself

The self is not something ready-made, but something in continuous formation through choice of action.

—JOHN DEWEY

Nick, an architect who has a Shy fear style, had never imagined acting in a play. "I don't have a dramatic bone in my body," he told me not long ago, "and the thought of getting up before an audience has always terrified me." But then his friend Sheila asked him to participate in a community theater production she was directing. How could Nick possibly honor his friend's request? How could he accept the challenge of being on stage? He protested, "I can't do this. I'd feel like I'm being led off to a firing squad. What if I forget my lines? What if I freeze up while everyone's watching?" As we discussed the situation, however, Nick realized that his part in the play would be truly small—only two lines totaling twelve words in two scenes. "What do I mean, I can't do it?" Nick asked himself in my presence. "Anybody could do *this* part, so why not me?"

After some trepidation—and more than a little cajoling by Sheila—Nick accepted the challenge. He joined her production, learned his lines, participated in the rehearsals, enjoyed the camaraderie, and did a good job on stage. Did his experience lead to a brilliant theatrical career? No. Was Nick disappointed? Not at all. On the contrary, he felt pleased that his efforts wouldn't continue past this one production, but he also surprised himself by enjoying it as much as he did. "That was quite an experience," Nick told me later. "It was my acting debut—and most likely my acting swan song, too—but I'm glad I did it. I'd never been through anything like that, and it was a good thing to have experienced."

Best of all, Nick learned a lot about himself in the process. He discovered that much of his initial resistance to the idea of acting wasn't the deep dread he'd suspected; it was a more superficial nervousness. During the production, he learned that stage fright is a common experience even among seasoned actors, and he learned ways to ease what he felt. He also found that he could tackle a challenge—one unlike anything he'd done before—and prevail. He not only acted in a play, he did a creditable job with his small part. Okay, so he confirmed his suspicion that he's not the next Tom Cruise, but that wasn't what Nick cared about. The process mattered more than the result because it strengthened his sense of self. Being part of the production expanded Nick's perceptions of who he is and what he can accomplish. Nick had strengthened his self muscle, and doing so has carried over into other challenges he will need to face in the future.

Not *Knowing Was Even More Frightening*

Here's another story—one that's dramatic in a different sense of the word. Camille, a homemaker all her life and someone who tends to be Compliant in her fear style, regarded herself as the last person in the world who could ever fly a plane. Her husband, Peter, is a business-man and licensed pilot. Peter and Camille own a four-seat Cessna that they use on business trips. So far so good. However, Peter has wor-ried for years about flying with his wife: if he ever became incapaci-tated while piloting the plane, the flight could end disastrously for both of them. For this reason, Peter requested that Camille learn to fly. She wouldn't need to become an accomplished pilot—only skilled enough to take over the plane and land it if necessary.

Camille found this whole scenario alarming. How could she ever learn to pilot a plane? She found even day-to-day driving stressful. Yet she also admitted that she was deeply fearful about the possibil-ity that her husband might suffer a heart attack or other health crisis while flying the Cessna. After Peter requested that she consider flight training, Camille wrestled with her emotions about the entire issue.

Eventually, though, she worked her way through to a decision. Business travel was a reality in her husband's life. Peter wasn't about to stop flying the plane, and she genuinely enjoyed accompanying him on his trips. Either they could continue traveling as in the past, gambling that no mishaps would occur, or she could open her mind to new possibilities as a hedge against crises in the future. Camille entered a flight training program a few weeks later. She learned the necessary skills and enjoyed flying the plane more than she'd ever thought possible. "It's not that I didn't find it scary," she confessed after acquiring her license. "In many ways flying *is* scary. But in other ways *not* knowing how to fly was even more frightening, so I had to take that step." "That step" was actually many separate tasks involved in mastering the various technical skills necessary to pilot a plane. That step was also Camille's willingness to challenge herself and build her self muscle—strengthening her belief in her own capabilities.

Here's what I'm suggesting: whatever your background and inter-ests, you can widen your range of abilities and "work out" to strengthen them. And the more skills and know-how you acquire, the more competent and confident you'll feel. If you can acquire the habit of taking a forward-moving action every now and then, the process will become more and more comfortable. My recommendation: develop the habit of doing tasks that challenge you. The specific tasks don't have to be hair-raising or life-threatening. You don't have to go skydiving or track tigers in Nepal. The challenges can be modest, safe experiences. What's important is for them to make you stretch your sense of who you are and what you can do. Try out an unfamiliar cuisine. Meet new people. Develop a new skill. Express your needs and concerns more directly than in the past. Whatever you do, push the envelope.

Here are some suggestions for how to get started.

Get into the Mood and Warm Up First

When working out or exercising, many of us set the mood before getting down to business. We change our clothes and ease into our routines before we do anything strenuous. Musicians do something similar by playing scales or exercises. Lovers do it by creating a romantic mood with music, candles, sexy clothes, and anything else that works. Working out the self muscle can benefit from a similar approach. Almost anything that keeps you focused and prevents a spiral of worry can be productive. Brew yourself a cup of tea. Put on a CD. Dress comfortably. Stretch. Get organized to do what you need to do. Much as kids need to settle down before they start their homework, we adults need to settle down, too.

Here's another analogy I'll make to sports and fitness: before you tackle a major new experience, warm up first. If necessary, build up your self muscle with numerous small steps rather than intimidating big ones.

Suppose that Nick, the architect I mentioned earlier, had aspirations of an amateur acting career. His small part in a community theater would have been a great first step, and he could follow up with similar small roles in other local productions. Down the road he might tackle bigger challenges—acting classes, voice coaching, auditions. Not only would he gain skills as an actor; he'd also diminish his fears by strengthening his self muscle. Warming up in this way builds your confidence and comfort levels and gets you "in shape."

The steps I'm suggesting will also help you stretch your reach. I know this from my own experience. I'm an avid tennis player. I enjoy the game and pride myself on having improved a lot over the years. One of the things I've learned from playing tennis is the importance of reaching for a ball even when it seems to be too far away to make the attempt. It still amazes me how many shots I get with a long reach and a broad step. I often make this comparison to dealing with fear-producing tasks and activities, and here's what I recommend. You may think that something you want to do is beyond your ability, but it may well be close enough for you to accomplish. Don't underestimate your reach. Part of building up your self muscle is learning to S-T-R-E-T-C-H.

Identify What You Find Fear-Inducing

Sometimes it's hard to know what muscles you need to strengthen. When playing sports or doing fitness training, it's best to consider what you're striving for so that you can work on the muscles that need attention. The same is true when taking action to overcome your fears. (The quizzes in chapter 1 of this book can be helpful in this regard.) When you can identify what really triggers your fear, you have a better chance of knowing which skills to focus on.

- If you're a Shy person, strengthening your self muscle means speaking up and reaching out to other people.

- For the Controlling person, it means tolerating situations in which you have to relinquish control—learning to delegate, easing off on perfectionism, and letting go of the need to orchestrate other people's lives.

- If you're Hypervigilant, it means responding to situations with more trust and faith and less agitation and worry.

- For the Compliant person, it means expressing your own needs and reflecting on what *you* want, not what others want you to do.

- If you're a Macho person, it means admitting your're afraid rather than concealing your fear with anger, intimidation, or stubbornness.

Throughout this chapter, I'll suggest other options that will help clarify these concepts.

Use Virtual Reality

In the past, performing a new and unfamiliar task meant just that: you simply went out and did it. Millions of people learned to drive by getting into a car with a parent or an instructor, then setting off. There are advantages to this method in some situations but major drawbacks in others, especially if the circumstances are risky—or if you feel they're risky. Fortunately, it's now possible to tackle many new experiences in a safer, more controlled environment. This can be beneficial for many people but especially for folks who are fearful. What I'm talking about is virtual reality, both of high-tech and low-tech sorts. For starters, here are three examples of high-tech virtual reality that can help you ease your fears and acquire skills for later use in life.

Learning to Save Her Sister's Life

Helene has been frightened by her sister Marla's diagnosis of heart disease but ambivalent about what she should do to help her. She worried that she'd never learn to master the skills of CPR or the use of an automated external defibrillator (AED), which might be crucial if Marla went into cardiac arrest. On the other hand, she was also uneasy about forgoing the chance to learn these skills, which might one day save her sister's life. When she finally decided to take a CPR course, she felt relieved to learn that the instructors relied on automated CPR mannequins, which helped Helene quickly learn the necessary skills. She also mastered the use of the AED by means of a computerized training simulator. The course wasn't as demanding or as strenuous as she expected. Helene is now confident that she can help Marla if her sister faces a cardiac emergency.

Back Behind the Wheel

During his teens, Nat suffered a serious auto accident that left him terrified of cars and unwilling to drive. Now in his late twenties, Nat feels that he must overcome this fear or suffer great damage to his professional career and social life. The problem: how to push past his accumulated fears and learn to drive again. After wrestling with this problem for years, Nat found a driver-training company that would instruct him initially by means of an automobile simulator. This device provided a computerized simulation of driving without ever leaving the training facility. The experience of simulated driving allowed Nat to lower his fear level, before acquiring the skills he needs to be behind the wheel of a real car.

Room by Room

Nora has always wanted to build a dream house. She and her husband, Freddy, now have sufficient money to undertake this project. What concerns both of them is that Nora, who's Controlling in her fear style and quick to admit that she's a perfectionist, will rack up a huge bill with the architects—and probably drive them crazy with her indecisiveness. She'll change her mind a thousand times before they even get around to sketching the plans. Nora worries about this problem but also dreads not having the chance to experiment with her ideas for the house. She solved her problem by acquiring a house design program for her computer. By means of this program, Nora can try out architectural ideas in a harmless, inexpensive way. The program even creates a virtual house that Nora can tour (and show off to friends) room by room.

Virtual reality doesn't have to be high-tech. There are wonderful low-tech kinds as well, some of which are even better and more adaptable than the newer electronic kinds.

Letters

Martin, a young high school science teacher, received a mixed first-year assessment from his supervisor. He wouldn't have minded hearing constructive criticism, but the supervising teacher's comments ignored Martin's substantial achievements, focusing instead on issues that stemmed from a personality conflict between the two men. During our conversations about his assessment, Martin expressed great anger about this situation, yet he felt reluctant to defend himself. "This is a terrible development," Martin told me. "I wanted to have a stellar first year in the classroom, and now I have this arrogant guy shooting me down practically before I'm off the runway! And his comments go straight into my permanent record."

I suggested to Martin that he take action, perhaps by means of a face-to-face conversation with the supervisor.

Martin, who tends toward a Shy fear style, found this recommendation unnerving. "Are you kidding? Me? Either I'll fall totally silent—or else I'll rant and rave and get myself fired!"

"Well, do you think you could make *some* sort of response?"

"I guess so, but I'm scared it'll backfire."

We ended up working out a plan. Since Martin felt too intimidated by his supervisor to confront him in person, he decided to write a rebuttal to his first-year assessment. This arrangement would have many advantages. First, writing a letter would allow Martin to think through his response on paper, which would allow his thoughtfulness and articulateness to come into full play. Second, it would allow Martin to respond to the supervisor's criticisms without interruption or manipulation that could happen during a face-to-face meeting. Third, it would fall within his rights as an employee to state his own case. Fourth, Martin's comments—not just the supervisor's criticism—would end up as part of his permanent record.

This arrangement may sound as if it's "only" writing a letter, but in important ways letter writing can be a kind of virtual reality, too. It allows Martin to visualize and experiment with his responses. He can confront the accusations against him and rebut them effectively. He can even imagine the arrogant supervisor in front of him, which may help Martin contemplate how to handle future confrontations with difficult people. In short, writing a letter lets Martin "think on paper," try out various scenarios for size, determine what best suits his purposes, and clarify his statements for strategic purposes.

Actually, Martin has two low-tech virtual reality options here. One option is a letter intended simply to let off steam; he won't actually send it. Martin can write anything he wants—make any accusations, state any demands, even rant and rave. He can use this option as a way of getting the anger he feels out of his system. A letter of this sort is a harmless, effective way to vent his feelings.

The other option is to use the letter as a means to think through the issues (as noted above) and to make a statement for legal and professional purposes. This is the kind of letter that he would actually send. For obvious reasons, Martin can still vent his fury in early drafts of the letter, if that seems cathartic, but later drafts—and certainly the draft that ultimately goes into the mailbox—should reflect Martin's long-term view of what he wants to accomplish in dealing with his supervisor.

In short, you can adapt this letter-writing technique to many purposes. It's a wonderful way to release tensions and ease fears. Writing a letter doesn't oblige you to send it. The recipient doesn't even have to be alive. In fact, writing a letter can be an especially satisfying way to express feelings about someone—or toward someone—who is no longer living. Releasing your frustrations in a letter to a deceased parent, sibling, spouse, or friend can be a powerful healing experience. The same holds true for keeping a journal or diary—a safe, easy, inexpensive, highly personal way to vent the emotions you feel and reach insights on paper.

Role Playing

Another useful form of low-tech virtual reality is role playing. I use variants of this technique in psychotherapy sessions with my patients. Role playing lets you try out certain kinds of experiences in a safe, controlled environment in the company of a trusted guide.

Jerri, 56 years old and Compliant in her fear style, has struggled for years with her older brother Ben regarding their mother's medical and personal difficulties. Their mother, Claire, is 83 and in progressively failing health. Claire still lives alone but requires more and more attention, most of which Jerri provides. Ben tells his sister that looking after their mother should be her responsibility, since "you live closer to her" and "you have more time." Jerri doesn't dispute either of these points, but she feels strongly that Ben presses the issues in this way primarily to avoid taking any responsibility at all. Attempts to discuss the situation often degenerate into pointless arguments. Jerri resents her brother's attitude yet dreads dealing with him so much that she usually capitulates to whatever arrangements he suggests, which invariably solidifies her caregiving role.

Role playing within the context of psychotherapy has allowed Jerri a way to vent her frustrations, explore future options, and learn better ways of dealing with her sibling conflict. It has also helped Jerri to be more confident since she has already clarified her thoughts and sorted through options before she speaks with her brother. Another wonderful benefit of role playing is that she doesn't start interactions with her brother in an agitated, anxious state, because she has rehearsed her opening statement.

To summarize, the benefits of role playing include:

- Actively preparing for situations you need to face in the future
- Expanding the number of ideas you have for dealing with situations
- Lowering levels of fear and tension
- Strategizing how to deal with other people, particularly difficult ones
- Rehearsing for upcoming discussions, conversations, or confrontations

Some kinds of role playing can also take place during group therapy. Jerri, who participated both in individual and group therapy, had the advantage of experiencing two additional types of virtual reality experiences, which enabled her to become much more confident when she spoke with her brother. First, she chose Barry, a male group member, to "play act" Ben. She briefly described Ben's character so that Barry would know how to play the part well. (With just a little narrative background, most people can do a phenomenal job simulating what another person might say in a specific circumstance.) Then Jerri chose Nora, a female group member whom she admired for her poise, to coach her whenever she felt intimidated or lost for words in her simulated conversation. These two approaches allowed Jerri to broaden her perspective, practice new modes of communication, and allay her fears.

Exposure Experience

Virtual reality is great preparation for learning to do what's necessary in a new environment, but eventually you need experience in the real world. Although firefighters can undergo endless training by means of films and classes, they'll learn best by being out in the field, fighting real fires. The same holds true for doctors doing procedures, lawyers trying cases, parents raising children, and people in many other fields doing their specialized kinds of work.

Hopefully, you will have received sufficient training in your own field before you are actually out on your own. Hopefully you'll be well prepared. You'll know how to handle the situations you face—except, of course, when you *don't*. Because sometimes you won't. I regret to say it, but it's true: blunders and mishaps may happen to you.

Joan remembers the first time she taught kids in her own classroom. She'd had experience as a student teacher, but that's very different from being thrown in front of thirty inner-city twelve-year-olds. "The situation was much harder than I ever thought," Joan admits. "Every night I went home discouraged, thinking I'd made a mistake. Maybe I shouldn't have gone into teaching. Some nights I cried myself to sleep, believing I'd never be able to manage a classroom. " Joan desperately needed to calm herself down and figure out what course of action to take.

She came up with two resolutions:

1. Cut herself some slack. She was a first-year teacher. How could she expect to know it all?

2. Discuss how to deal with the discipline problems in her classroom with her principal and other, more experienced teachers.

There's no substitute for real-life experience. No classroom simulations could prepare Joan for the realities of working in a high-stress environment. Ultimately, though, she got the experience she needed and went on to become a first-rate teacher.

Guided Imagery

Although it's not usually considered a form of virtual reality, guided imagery is a way of exploring reality, this time in the safety of your own mind. Guided imagery can help you imagine a safe place to grow a stronger self. It's also a remarkably effective way to calm the body, quiet the mind, and set aside concerns that are nagging at you.

You can create imagery on your own that can calm you, encourage you, and reassure you. Here is the imagery that Melissa uses to reassure herself: "When I feel that everything is just too much, I retreat (in my imagination) to a beautiful, comfortable, well-decorated cocoon. It's located high up on top of a redwood tree, overlooking a valley so I'm not going to have any neighbors come by to pester me. In this sanctuary, I can relax and shield myself from any criticism or aspersions. When I arrive at the cocoon, I generally feel like a little nobody caterpillar. But if I take the time I need, I emerge feeling like a lovely, graceful, agile butterfly who can fly wherever I want and can alight wherever I please."

I often use guided imagery with my patients. Many of them find this technique useful as a way of easing either a general sense of fearfulness or specific fears they're struggling with.

Before I give you an example, though, I want to offer a few general comments about how to set the stage for this experience:

- Pick a quiet, relaxing place to perform the exercise. It's less likely to be effective if you're struggling to ignore background noise or other distractions.

- Select a time for guided imagery when you're not too physically tired or subject to outside interruptions.

- It's most effective if you do guided imagery with your eyes closed. For this reason, *reading* what follows isn't the ideal way to proceed when you do the exercise itself. I suggest that you either have someone read you the sequence of steps in a slow, relaxed, comforting voice, or else tape the instructions yourself for later playback.

Exercise: Use Guided Imagery

What follows is a guided imagery to diminish stress and create a "safe place" within the mind that can become a haven in the future.

1. Find a comfortable position. Close your eyes. Turn your attention away from outside events and notice how your body is feeling.

2. If you feel any discomfort, see if you can make yourself more comfortable.

3. Focus your attention on your breathing. Inhale slowly and exhale slowly, imagining that each breath is like a gentle wave on the shore, enhancing your energy as you inhale, eliminating stress as you exhale.

4. Now imagine that you find yourself in a setting where you feel deeply relaxed. This may be a place you've actually visited—a beautiful beach, a lovely meadow, a grand mountain vista—or it could be a place you're imagining with your mind's eye.

5. Take a few moments to look around at your surroundings in your mind. What do you see? What do you hear? What is it about this place that makes you feel so comfortable?

6. Be aware that you're feeling more and more relaxed. Your body is letting go of any tension you were holding on to. Your mind is letting go of any worries that have been nagging at you. You don't have to do anything. You don't have to take care of anything. You can just let yourself *be* in this safe, nurturing environment.

7. With your eyes still closed, take another look around at where you are. Notice something that's particularly soothing, something you didn't notice right away. See what it is that you find comforting about whatever you've observed.

8. Now be aware of a specific sound that you hear, a sound that is calming and comforting to you, a sound that brings a smile to your face.

9. Notice that there's a smell in the air that's soothing—a fragrant breeze, the scent of flowers, or the clear, clean air itself.

10. Inhale slowly once again. Exhale slowly. Take a mental snapshot of the whole imagery so you'll remember it well. Take your time to say good-bye to this wonderful place that has been nourishing you. Remind yourself that you can come back here whenever you please. Give yourself a few moments to appreciate this unique experience.

11. Whenever you're ready, open your eyes and return to the room you're in.

How do you feel? What do you want to remember from this experience?

Fake It Till You Make It

Courage is the art of being the only one who knows you're scared to death.

—Earl Wilson

Here's one of life's biggest secrets: you don't have to feel confident on the inside to look confident on the outside. In fact, many of the world's most accomplished people feel shy, shaky, even terrified as they go about achieving their great deeds. This is true for many renowned actors, singers, business people, politicians, teachers, athletes, and others.

Melinda, a 35-year-old Shy woman I've worked with, recently described her use of this technique. "I've learned that nobody has to know how much you're shaking or how much you doubt yourself—unless you choose to let them in on your secret. You don't have to advertise your fears or your lack of confidence. I used to think that my insecurities were visible to everybody, but now I'm amazed at how often people mistake my shyness for strength and my silence for competence."

The truth is, you can pretend not to be afraid even if you're frightened out of your wits, and doing so is half the task of learning to overcome your fears. Difficult? Probably. Worthwhile? Definitely. For if you can "go through the motions" for a while, you'll not only accomplish what you've set out to do—you'll also discover that after awhile, this pretend courage will most likely become your reality. In short, you can "fake it till you make it."

Seth, starting his first job right after college, discovered that his employer had assumed he'd be familiar with a particular business spreadsheet program. In fact, Seth hadn't worked with this program, though he'd never claimed otherwise. Fearful that revealing his ignorance outright would scuttle his job on the spot, Seth told a little white lie, saying that he'd used this program only occasionally. He then asked a friend to bring him up to speed on the program after work. Seth is a quick study with computer technology, so he got the hang of the new spreadsheet and settled into his job without this issue hanging over him for long.

Liz is another example of how to fake it till you make it. A nurse by training, she has a managerial role within a large hospital and frequently presents inservices to ward nurses and other personnel. Liz knows her material, has a passion for nursing, and enjoys teaching. Like most of us, though, she's nervous about public speaking and especially dreads presenting to groups larger than eight or ten people. So how does she manage to cope with a role she finds nervewracking? "A few years ago I was required to watch a videotape of a presentation I'd given," she told me. "I was discussing some complex nursing issues, and I felt scared to death about covering the material *and* holding myself together. To make matters even worse, someone stuck this video camera in my face, making me feel even more self-conscious! But you know what? When I watched the videotape the next day, you couldn't see how jittery and jumpy I was feeling. You couldn't hear the quaver in my voice or see that my palms were sweaty. It looked like I was pretty much in control. I didn't feel that way, but I guess I was the only person who knew the truth, so after that I'd just go about my business and let people give me the benefit of the doubt."

The Value of Faking It Till You Make It

If you want a quality, act as if you already had it. Try the "as if" technique.

—WILLIAM JAMES

The people around you probably don't even know that you're scared. You may feel that you're red in the face, sweating profusely or your heart is pounding, but other folks probably aren't aware of what seems so obvious to you. Your self-consciousness makes you think your appearance is more conspicuous than it really is. Just quietly go about your business, Liz advises. If you're like most people, you're probably your own toughest critic. Cut yourself some slack. The odds are that you look better and sound better than you imagine. You're most likely the only person expecting you to be perfect.

Faking it till you make it allows you an opportunity to pick up new skills. With experience, persistence, and time, you'll be surprised by how much knowledge you can acquire and how much confidence you can develop. Fear may be self-perpetuating, but so is confidence. The truth is that the more skills you have under your belt, the more easily you'll tackle new ones in the future, until one day what seems impossible for you now will seem like child's play. You don't know what you can do until you try it.

Mild nervousness can actually help you. Athletes, musicians, actors, political figures, public speakers, and others who must perform under pressure are all boosted by low-level stress. It's true that excessive anxiety and nervousness may work against you, but having a few butterflies in your stomach may actually work in your favor. So if you're feeling wound up, on edge, or shaky, don't let that stop you—mild or moderate stress may actually work to your advantage.

Anticipatory anxiety is often worse than the actual experience you'll face. Time after time I hear people say, after the experience is over, "It wasn't as bad as I thought it would be." This statement holds true for experiences as varied as learning to swim, giving a speech, meeting new people, starting a new job, serving on a jury, asking for a raise— one thing after another. If you can fake it till you make it, you gain an opportunity to step beyond your fear, get immersed in the task at hand, and proceed.

One last thing. Faking it does *not* mean that you're doing anything shady. It doesn't mean you're defrauding other people. All it means is that you're camouflaging your insecurities rather than advertising them to the world. Like everyone else, you're in the process of continual growth and development. If you prefer not to share with everyone that you're a novice or that you feel like a rookie, so be it. Just go about doing what's new, challenging, uncomfortable, or outright frightening, and you'll find your life enriched in a way that wouldn't be possible if you consistently avoid these challenges.

Sometimes I hear my patients (as well as other people) say, "I can't imagine being . . ." or "I can't imagine doing . . . ." Fill in the blank. Yes, it's hard to imagine being or doing many things. Many aspects of life are intimidating, even threatening. But as I see it, part of the goal each of us faces is precisely to imagine being more, doing more, becoming more than we are now. Don't stifle your imagination. "Imagination," wrote Norman Vincent Peale, "is the true magic carpet." Keep your imagination fresh. Despite your fear, color outside the lines. If people couldn't imagine doing more:

- Glenn would never have traveled to Russia.
- Brian would never have started his own business.
- Adam would never have had an adult Bar Mitzvah.
- Danny would never have organized a fund raiser.
- Ron would never have gotten his doctorate.
- Barbara would never be teaching yoga.
- I would never be writing this book.

My recommendation: give yourself a chance to try new things. You're not sure exactly what you're doing? Welcome to the human race. Take a shot at it anyway. Allow yourself room to grow. Do your best. And while doing so, go ahead and pretend you're confident about what you're doing. If you act as if you're not afraid even when you are, what you pretend may well become the truth.

12

Steps for Doing
One Gutsy Thing

People grow through experience if they meet life honestly and courageously. This is how character is built.

—ELEANOR ROOSEVELT

WHAT I'VE SAID SO FAR MAY SOUND DAUNTING. You may feel it's difficult to strengthen your "self muscle" when you never even knew you had one. You may find it hard to fake it till you make it when your knees are shaking. When every cell in your body seems to be crying out *I don't know what I'm doing*, the changes I'm recommending may seem like a major challenge.

But here's the good news. You don't have to tackle big changes at the outset. The important thing is simply to get going. And one way to do so is to adopt the principle of One Gutsy Thing.

The Concept of OGT

Many years ago, I did a series of speaking engagements with my friend Sheila Peck, sponsored by a group called the Center for Women and Achievement. After our presentation, we would interview one woman about what she regarded as her One Gutsy Thing and ask her to describe how she had mustered the courage to do whatever that had been. Sometimes the OGT, as the participants began to call it, had to do with career skills, such as going back to college or getting a better job. At other times it related to personal situations. One interview that brought tears to most people's eyes was when Fran, a timid, tiny woman, finally had the guts to confront her authoritarian father, telling him, "You didn't treat me right when I was a kid. You had no right to yell at me the way you did and call me stupid and tell me I was ugly. You owe me an apology."

These women came to the seminars because they recognized that the actions they took, *despite feeling fear in their gut*, were ways for them to build integrity and personal power. In front of a roomful of people, they didn't use that old excuse "I'm uncomfortable with that" to avoid important action.

Here's the way one Compliant woman put it: "I was the peacemaker in my family. I never wanted to create waves. I used to joke about my fear of displeasing others by saying, 'Some of my friends are for it, some are against it, and I'm with my friends.' But now that I look back on the way I used to live, it seems pathetic. I never had an opinion, never did anything out of the ordinary, never took a chance. I was drowning in caution and starved for adventure. I'm so proud of how far I've come."

Just as fear comes in all sizes, the same is true for doing One Gutsy Thing. Not everyone starts to swim by jumping right into the pool; some of us enter the water gradually, sometimes one baby step at a time. But it doesn't really matter how you get into the pool of life—all that matters is that you *do* get in. Don't look over your shoulder to compare yourself with others. What's a big deal for you may be effortless for someone else, and what's a challenge to someone else may be a piece of cake for you.

Your OGT can be practically anything. What seems gutsy often relates to your fear style. If you're a Shy person, your OGT will probably be a social experience, such as going to a wedding where you know only the bride or the groom. If you're a Controlling person, your OGT will likely relate to relinquishing control, such as letting your spouse plan the family vacation. Here are a few other examples:

- Go to your first Weight Watchers meeting.

- Enroll in a graduate program.

- Take up a new sport.
- Learn to dance.
- Travel overseas.
- Confront your parent/spouse/ex-spouse/sibling about a disagreement.
- Leave your child with a baby-sitter.
- Decide to enter psychotherapy.
- Decide to end psychotherapy.
- Learn a new language.
- Start a new job.
- Quit a boring but well-paying job.

OGT—Emily's Story

Emily had always dreamed of attending college even though no one else in her family had any higher education. Her parents made it clear that they didn't support her interest. During high school her father repeatedly told her, "Why bother with college? You're just going to get married and have kids, so all that money will be wasted." Partly because of her Compliant fear style, she took this message to heart, got a job right out of high school, got married, and had three kids. Yet she always regretted her decision not to attend college.

Now forty-nine years old, with her kids grown and out of the house, Emily has doubled back on the issue of a college degree. Her husband, Gary, is vaguely supportive but hasn't done much to encourage her. Her boss indicates that if she earns a B.A. degree, her salary will increase. Emily feels torn by conflicting advice and worries that she's "not up for this" and that "maybe it's too late." She's uncertain about what to do, yet she dreads the possibility of missing out again. She knows several other women who have tackled midlife degree programs, and she doesn't want to skip an opportunity that might not come again. "But I still don't see how to pull this off," she said. "If I'm holding down a job, a B.A. degree would take me at least eight years! Can I really manage that? And can we afford it?"

"Why not start with one course?" I suggested.

"Just one course? Can you do that?"

"Yes," I told her. "You don't have to matriculate at the beginning. You can take a course this semester to see how you like it."

Emboldened by this information, Emily contacted her local community college, obtained a catalogue, explored her options, and eventually signed up for a course. The college turned out to be more flexible than she'd expected, with online courses, evening classes, credits for life experiences, and other options geared toward an adult-ed student population. The first course led to another. Emily soon formulated a plan for getting her degree in a timely manner, and now the end is in sight. She's a year away from finishing her B.A. degree in business administration.

Fear and Frustration

Here's another example. Leo feels increasingly frustrated with his boss, Matthew, whose temper can get out of control. Leo has contemplated confronting Matthew but hesitates, fearing that he'll lose his job. "I need to do something," he told me at one point, "but I don't know what that should be." To complicate matters, Leo's older brother has ridiculed him for his passivity, scolding him for letting Matthew use him "like a doormat." The tensions that Leo feels over this situation have become unbearable.

I'd like to say that Leo's situation has a simple resolution, but it doesn't. I'm not entirely sure what will come of it, but I do know that Leo will simmer in a complex broth of frustrations unless he decides to take some sort of action. Will he tackle the whole situation all at once? Probably not. I'm not sure that would be a good idea even if he suddenly decided to do it. What's more likely—and what would make good sense—would be if Leo decided to do One Gutsy Thing.

This could take one or more of several different forms. He could start psychotherapy to learn how to become more confrontative. He could take an assertiveness training seminar. He could request a meeting with someone in the human resources department at his company. He could explore his options for finding a different job. Each of these alternatives would have advantages and disadvantages. What's certain, however, is that Leo will feel increasingly frustrated if he does nothing at all.

What concerns me about this type of situation is the risk of *habitually* avoiding action. As we've discussed throughout this book, people sometimes feel they can't take action because they're too afraid or nervous. So they don't take action. Over time, avoidance becomes their coping style. As a short-term, occasional strategy, avoidance sometimes has its merits. But as a long-term, habitual strategy, it has an abundance of drawbacks.

Despite, Even Because of, Fear

> *Do not be too timid and squeamish about your actions. All life is an experiment. The more experiments you make, the better.*
>
> —Ralph Waldo Emerson

I suggest an alternate approach to the avoidance strategy. You can take action despite fear—sometimes even *because* of fear. You can admit, "This situation scares me. I'm afraid of what may happen, I hate that I feel so nervous, but I'm going to take action anyway." Taking this approach means that even though you feel the fear, it doesn't dictate or control your behavior.

Perhaps you're still doubtful—you think you're not ready for all this action-oriented stuff. Maybe you're right. But before you close the door to doing One Gutsy Thing, reflect on the following questions:

- If you're afraid of what will happen tomorrow, why not do something today that makes you feel more confident?
- If you're afraid of being assertive with your kids, why not take a parenting course?
- If you're afraid of extensive travel, why not take one brief trip?
- If you're afraid of asking for directions, why not try asking someone with a friendly face and see what happens?
- If you're afraid of learning a new skill in a public setting, why not purchase one of the "For Dummies™" books and explore the subject first?
- If you're afraid to give up micromanaging everyone in your family, why not try to simply let them handle one thing on their own?

- If you're afraid of marriage counseling, why not try one session and see what happens?

- If you're afraid of intimacy, why not confide that to someone you feel close to?

- If you're afraid of committing a social faux pas, why not commit one on purpose to see if the results are really so terrible?

- If you're afraid to give up smoking, why not try it for just one day?

- If you're afraid to make a difficult phone call, why not rehearse your opening sentence before you make the call?

- If you're afraid of dying, why not try living—fully—today?

Doing One Gutsy Thing won't put all your fears to rest. It can, however, unlock a door that's been locked far too long. And once that door is unlocked, you can open it a crack. Then give yourself the green light to open the door even wider. From there it's not so difficult to open it all the way, step through to the other side, and start exploring the big, beautiful world beyond.

Learn from the Messages in Children's Stories

I often use the messages that lie embedded within children's stories to emphasize an important point. Every first-rate children's story has a thoughtful theme—for adults as well as children. These stories work on many levels; a child can understand the basic message of the story, while adults can explore a deeper meaning.

My favorite children's book is *The Wizard of Oz*. A central theme of L. Frank Baum's classic book is that each of the major characters is looking for something that he or she doesn't have. Dorothy is searching for a sense of belonging (home); the Scarecrow for a brain; the Cowardly Lion for courage; the Tin Man for a heart. They have no idea how to get what they want, so they look for someone wiser to give it to them. But no matter how polite they are, how much they plead, or how upset they get, the Wizard doesn't grant their wishes.

Instead, he sends them out into the world to do a task—to bring back the broomstick of the Wicked Witch of the West.

Now comes the part of the story that many people miss. Dorothy, who's searching for a sense of belonging, is the person who keeps everyone together. The Scarecrow, who has no brains, thinks up the plan. The Cowardly Lion, who has no courage, leads the group on their adventure. The Tin Man, who has no heart, looks after the others caringly. As each of these four characters does his or her One Gutsy Thing, *they are becoming who they want to be.*

But they still don't quite get it. So they return to the Wizard to have him keep his end of the bargain. The Wizard, once he's been unmasked as merely a man, not a wizard, gives each one a *symbol*: Dorothy, the action she needs to take to go home again; the Scarecrow, a diploma; the Cowardly Lion, a medal; and the Tin Man, a heart. The Wizard emphasizes to the four travelers that these symbols aren't the real thing; they are only *reminders* of what they have achieved through their efforts. A diploma doesn't make you smart; a satin heart doesn't make you loving; a medal doesn't make you brave. It's when the characters carry out their tasks—when they *take action*—that they gain the courage, the wisdom, the intelligence, and the belonging. Contrary to popular assumptions, Baum's message is not that we had it inside us all along, but rather that we have the *potential* within us. And we activate that potential when we take action.

Many other books for children and young adults also instill the message that you can overcome fear and triumph over adversity by taking action. No doubt you have your own favorite childhood tales. Think about what those books were and what message you took from them. Do you think that the message could still be useful now as a way of mastering your fears and lifting your burdens?

Although some people would regard children's books as "only" part of their formative years, that's exactly what makes them so powerful. The stories we remember become part of our mental structure; they teach us important values, open our minds to new ideas, and encourage us to believe in ourselves. I strongly recommend that you revisit the children's books that resonated during your childhood—or during the years of parenting your own kids. Take them to heart and find strength in their messages.

Exercise: Find the Message in Your Old Favorites

Answer these three questions:

1. When you were a child, what were your favorite books?

_____

_____

_____

2. What was the major message for you in those books?

_____

_____

_____

3. How do you think that message relates to your life today?

_____

_____

_____

For Julie, the most meaningful book she read as a child is one whose name she can't even remember now. It was the story of a young girl who wanted to play baseball but wasn't allowed to simply because she was a girl. In the book, everyone knew girls can't play baseball. So the main character hid her long hair under her baseball cap and went down to the ballpark anyway. She practiced with the boys and got good at the game. When the time came for the big game, she went up to bat and hit a whopper. As she flew past third base, her cap came off, revealing her pigtails. By that time, though, everyone was cheering for her, and they never stopped.

Julie loved this book not only for the story itself but also for its message. As a bright but timid girl, she resented the barriers she faced while growing up. This book emboldened her with its message: Don't let anybody tell you that you can't do what matters to you. If you want something, go for it. The very people who will try to stop you today will congratulate you tomorrow.

Further Suggestions for Taking Action

The only way to even approach doing something perfectly is through experience, and experience is the name everyone gives to their mistakes.

—Oscar Wilde

There are many other ways in which taking action will help you overcome your fears, acquire new experiences, and widen the scope of your life. Here are a scattering of other suggestions that I hope you'll find useful.

Deliberately Do Something in a Different Way

Prove to yourself that you can do things differently by deliberately changing how and when you do a task. Modify your routine. Take a new route. Respond to a comment in an unusual way. Say yes to something that you usually answer no to. When you're always in control, life is predictable, safe, and—boring. See if you can take a risk and let go of the control. Most things will turn out just fine. And in the rare situation in which something bad happens, trust that you'll be able to deal with it anyway, becoming stronger and wiser as a result of the experience.

Sometimes an upcoming situation seems so threatening that you can't imagine dealing with it at all. But it's important not to see things in all-or-nothing terms. What may seem an alarming, overwhelming, even impossible task may be one you can modify and make more manageable.

To alleviate your fears, sometimes simply changing the environment will do the trick. Jake dealt with this issue while vacationing with his family at a Cape Cod town called Truro. Although he's an adequate swimmer, Jake felt alarmed by the rough surf on the ocean beaches, and he disliked the cold North Atlantic, which left him chilled within a few minutes in the water. His discomfort intensified as he worried about his children, aged ten and six, and imagined the dangers that might befall them at the beach. Jake's alarm quickly made him miserable and frustrated the other members of his family.

Jake's concerns for his own safety, and for his children's, weren't altogether unwarranted. In fact, the North Atlantic is chilly, and the Cape's ocean beaches are known to have unpredictable currents and undertows. Even so, his acute fears definitely interfered with his family's ability to have a good time while on vacation. After evaluating the options, however, Jake and his wife came up with an alternate plan: they'd switch from the ocean beaches to the nearby beaches on Cape Cod Bay. At Truro the Cape is only a few miles wide, so it's easy to drive that short distance to the other side. The conditions there quickly met Jake's needs. The beaches are flatter, the surf is gentler, and the water is ten or fifteen degrees warmer than in the Atlantic. Jake found that under these less challenging conditions, he relaxed, felt less apprehensive, and quickly started to enjoy himself. The bay beaches pleased his kids, too, since they could play with less stringent supervision.

It's important to appreciate that most situations aren't "either/or." You can often change aspects of what you're dealing with; you don't need to choose between tolerating the whole package or tossing it out altogether. If Jake had focused only on "either/or," he could have either scuttled the entire beach vacation or else gritted his teeth and suffered through the activities that caused him to feel fear and discomfort. Instead, he and his wife changed specific conditions: they selected a different beach that offered greater physical comfort and reduced risk.

Don't Just Wish—Make It Happen

How many times have your fears prevented you from taking action on something you wanted to do? When Lila discovered that I've been writing a column for many years, she was impressed. "I wish I had your talent," she said wistfully. "I've always been interested in writing, but I don't think I'm creative—I'm not really good at expressing myself."

"Tell me what you would write about, if you could," I responded.

"I'd want to tell my secrets," Lila admitted. "There's so much inside of me bursting to come out. I really should put my thoughts on paper, but I'm very sensitive, and I have a great fear that my writing would be shot down immediately if I tried."

I felt compassion for Lila, because I know that she, like many others, restricts her actions because of a double whammy—fear of failure plus a high sensitivity to criticism.

I asked Lila to remember whether she was creative as a child. Her demeanor changed at once. "Oh yes," she said. "I had so much fun with my sister. Sometimes we'd dress up like fancy ladies having tea. Sometimes we acted out a Mary Poppins story, always with a new adventure."

I gazed at Lila and wondered what she would be like today if she were not so fearful of being judged as inadequate. If, instead of inhibiting an action because of the fear, she took an action in spite of the fear. If, instead of feeling envious of others' achievements, she turned that energy into working on her own achievements.

Many talents, interests, and desires have wilted away because people do not act on them. Instead of looking back and kicking yourself because you haven't done what you wanted to do, how about changing your "should haves" to "I'm so glad I did this"? Here are a few people I know who are so much happier now because they acted on their desires:

- For Sandy, it was a desire to play the piano.
- For Marc, it was a wish to sing in a choral group.
- For Zoë, it was a yearning to be close to her grandson.
- For Lori, it was a wish to find the 33-year-old daughter she had given up for adoption at birth.
- For Alex, it was a longing to make peace with his brother before he died.
- For Rennie, it was an urge to get a better job.

What is it for you?

Many people worry about shortcomings, difficulties, and outright failure as they consider taking on new activities. They dread messing up or making fools of themselves. They second-guess every possible eventuality in every new endeavor, which bogs them down in endless conjecture before they take a single step. ("I'll drop the ball." "I won't learn the material." "I'll do it wrong." "I'll stammer/lose my place/forget my lines." "I'll let the team down." "I'll fall apart under pressure.) I recommend that, instead of letting your excuses run the show, you give your new behavior a chance. It won't be as difficult as you think if you recognize that:

- Whatever problem it is that you're worried about, it probably won't happen.

- If some aspect of this new activity does go badly, it probably won't be so awful.

- Even if the situation is awful, you'll get through it—this too shall pass, and you'll learn from the experience and move on.

You can't be brave if you've only had wonderful things happen to you.

—MARY TYLER MOORE

Sometimes there's a tendency to avoid action because life seems unfair. Well, of course life is unfair. Maybe you don't have some of the advantages that others have, or you lack the fearless nature that your friend has. But so what? Compared to most people throughout history and in most of the contemporary world, there's an excellent chance that overall, you've lucked out in life. You could be living in a country where you can't speak up, can't get an education, or can't travel freely. You could be living in poverty, or you could be constrained by political oppression or rigid racism or sexism. Life is unfair, but if you don't compare yourself to the celebrities you envy or the neighbors who seem to have everything, you'll recognize that your lot in life could have been a lot worse.

I highlight this issue of unfairness because this attitude can trip you up. There's a risk that you'll spend so much time feeling resentful that you'll give up taking action before you even get started.

My advice: go ahead and get your feet wet. Ultimately all new tasks require making the plunge. In many (if not most) settings, you'll have people to help you get started and cheer you on. You'll probably be far more critical about your performance than are the people showing you the ropes. So I recommend that you take a deep breath, don't focus on your fears, and just get started. This suggestion applies to sports, public speaking, dancing, jobs, volunteer work, school, technology, and almost everything else.

Exercise: Act on Your Interests

1. Write down an interest, talent, or desire that you want to act on. Even if you're not exactly sure what it is, write something down.

_____

_____

_____

2. Write down one thing you might do (not _think about_, but _do_) to enlarge the interest, enrich the talent, or satisfy the desire. For writing, it might mean taking a writing course. For making a relationship more intimate, you might set a date for getting together, or compose a heartfelt note.

_____

_____

_____

_____

3. Now imagine that you actually implemented what you wrote in question 2. Imagine that you took the action, even if it was tough, frightening, or more difficult than you thought. Picture yourself learning, thriving, and doing what you were afraid of. Write down what it feels like to accomplish what you set out to do.

_____

_____

_____

_____

4. How can you encourage yourself to continue the path of action that you started?

_____

_____

_____

_____

5. How do you think you will feel if you continue on this path of action until you actually get what you want?

_____

_____

_____

6. Now, imagine that something inhibits you from taking or continuing the action until completion. What might stop or restrain you?

_____

_____

_____

If you are thinking that you stop yourself because
- I don't have the time.
- I don't have the money.
- I don't have the energy.
- I don't have the talent.
- I don't know how.

Scratch these off your list. Even if they are partially true, they aren't the real reason. (As Marilyn Monroe once said, "I wasn't the prettiest, I wasn't the most talented. I simply wanted it more than anyone else.")

7. Dig deeper and find out what real fear is impeding your progress. Write it down.

_____

_____

_____

8. Now, instead of reinforcing that fear, write down a few affirmations that will encourage you to move beyond that fear. (For Lila, her fear was "I won't be good enough; I'll make a fool of myself." Her affirmations were "I can be patient with myself. I am getting better; I don't need to be perfect.")

_____

_____

_____

Differentiate Trying to Do Something from Actually Doing It

When people feel resistance to doing something, they often say they will *try to* do something rather than take the action and do it. The resistance is usually covering up a fear. The inability to differentiate between these two approaches can confound your best intentions.

Both Jason and Gabe lost their jobs when their company made personnel cuts. Since the layoffs occurred, Jason has been "trying" to get a job. He's looked online and in the classified ads but has found nothing that interests him. Gabe has updated his résumé, sent out ten résumés a week, networked with colleagues, prepared for interviews, and read two books on effective self-marketing. Notice the difference in action. Jason is simply trying to do something—a vague, often ineffective notion—while Gabe has taken specific, aggressive steps to solve his employment problem. My recommendation: differentiate between what you are trying to do and what you are actually doing.

It's true that there are some things you can legitimately try to do yet not accomplish. Remember freeing yourself from the outcome? Ben wanted to ask Lisa out on a date. He could *try* to get her to say yes, but he couldn't *make* her say yes. Trying is a valid concept when you're actually taking the action but the outcome isn't totally in your control. That said, all the trying in the world won't make anything happen if your trying is in reality, thinking without doing, making a half-hearted attempt, or neglecting to keep your promises.

Exercise: Don't Just Try—Do It!

1. What action do you think would be beneficial for you to take, but somehow you keep putting it off?

_____

_____

_____

2. Notice the ways you avoid doing it. Perhaps it might be that you believe you're trying but you have no plan of action. Or perhaps you say you'll do it later but later never comes. Or perhaps instead of telling yourself I'll do it, you say maybe I'll do it, or I wish I could do it, or I'd like to be able to do it. Notice that you're using a lot of tentative, vague words. Write down your most familiar pattern of resisting action.

_____

_____

_____

3. What's the fear behind your resistance? How do you feel about yourself when you avoid the action?

_____

_____

_____

4. Rewrite your statement from question 1, making it more definite and action-oriented. State definitively *what* you will do, *when* you will do it, and *how* you will do it.

_____

_____

_____

5. If you carry through on your action, how do you think you will feel about yourself? How will it affect your self muscle?

_____

_____

_____

Here's an example of how Lori did this exercise.

Lori, who wanted to locate the now-grown woman she gave up for adoption at birth, used this exercise to clarify what she could do to take action rather than just try to do it.

1. I want to contact the adoption agency I worked with.

2. I keep saying I'll do it later, but later never comes.

3. The fear is that if I find my daughter, she'll reject me. I would feel absolutely awful about that. Yet I feel I have no backbone when I keep putting it off.

4. If I were definite about my statement I would change it to: "I promise myself I'll call the agency before the end of this week."

5. If I carried it out, I'd feel damn good about myself. That self muscle you're speaking about would be strengthened. If I broke through the wall of fear I have, I'd look in the mirror and see a self-respecting woman.

Taking action doesn't settle all issues or solve all problems; however, it usually helps you move from a *complaint* position to a *solution-oriented* position. In complaint mode, you may feel like a victim: "I can't get a job," "I can't talk to her," "I can't stay calm." But when you take action, you move to a solution mode: "I'm seeing a career counselor now," "I'm taking an assertiveness training course," "I've enrolled in a yoga class." Even when you take action, you may not always get what you want, but at least it will get you moving in the right direction.

Use the Power of Paradox

Sometimes when you try too hard to change a pattern, it just doesn't work. Indeed, trying harder may even make the pattern worse—more bothersome or more frequent. At these times, it's best to acknowledge the power of paradox.

A paradox is a contradictory statement that nevertheless is true. Here are a few examples:

- You may be more tired at the end of a day in which you've done nothing than when you've been really busy.

- The more aware and educated you are, the more ignorant you may feel.

- The more you try to control someone, the more out of control you may feel—and actually become.

- Use all your energy to stay afloat in deep water and you have a better chance of drowning than if you relax your body.

- Try hard to make people like you and they don't; just be yourself and your chances will improve.

The power of paradoxical thinking is particularly useful when you feel stuck, afraid, and don't know what else to do.

Mary, who's Hypervigilant, has recently suffered three episodes of intense panic. Each time she felt embarrassed and frustrated by her emotional reactions, especially because she had to excuse herself abruptly and leave work. The next day, she'd make up a story about feeling sick to her stomach. She was worried that if her colleagues knew how anxious she was, they wouldn't understand, for outwardly she appeared to be a confident person.

But Mary's dilemma grew worse. The more she worried about being overcome with fear at work, the more fearful she became. At this point I suggested to her that the next time she was with colleagues, she should deliberately try to experience the panic that had been affecting her.

Her reaction was intense. "What do you mean?" she asked me. "That's insane. I dread having an attack and you want me to *make* myself have one?"

"That's right," I responded. "Just preplan your fear attack and see what happens."

As you might imagine, Mary was pleasantly surprised. When she stopped trying so hard to avoid the fear and let go of her need to control the fear, she relaxed and began to feel more at ease.

If you continue to struggle with a problem that you can't fix, it may be time to use a paradoxical approach. Stop trying to make things better. See if you can reverse direction and go *with* the problem instead of against it.

Keep Things Simple

'Tis the gift to be simple, 'tis the gift to be free.

—Shaker song

Many fearful people overwhelm themselves by worrying about a hundred and one things that may go wrong, or prove alarming. The surest way to frighten yourself is to pile on all the potential problems in the world. Instead, I recommend that at any one time, you deliberately limit the number of contingencies you face. Keep things simple.

There's something I like about small numbers, especially the numbers one, two, and three. There are many instances in which trying to manage more than three things at once creates unnecessary stress. I've organized my life so that I never, well hardly ever, have more than three things to do on my priority list. And often three is a lot.

Listen to the difference between these two scenarios:

Scenario A. "I'm always running around trying to get a hundred and one things done all day, and I never fail to forget something. After a busy day of trying to take care of everything, my husband usually dumps another task or two on me. It's just too much. Stop the world, I want to get off!"

Scenario B. "Today I've scheduled three things I'd like to take care of. The first is X, the second is Y, and—if I have time—I'll see if I get to Z. When I get home, if my husband wants something else taken care of, I'll put that on the schedule for tomorrow. Or maybe I'll nudge him into taking care of it himself."

Scenario A leaves the tasks to do completely open-ended; there's no limit to the things you need to take care of. By comparison, Scenario B creates a nice balance for your day without driving yourself crazy or acting as though everything on the agenda is urgent. What you can get to, you'll get to. The rest will follow.

Get Organized

What do *disordered, messy, mixed-up, scattered, scrambled,* and *all-over-the-place* have in common? These words all suggest confusion, chaos, bewilderment—great ingredients for a fear cocktail. If your space is cluttered and you can't find your belongings, what do you imagine the results will be? You're right: tension, tightness, worry, fear. Or, as Amanda says, "I'm losing things left and right. I can't keep track of anything, can't sleep, can't get anything done."

If you want to be successful in the actions you take, you have to develop an ability to get organized. This is obviously a complex issue, one that involves creating order out of chaos, plans out of anarchy, goals out of dreams. This isn't a book about getting organized, but it might be a good idea for you to buy one. What I want to stress here, however, is that you don't have to be a neat freak, but too much disorder, too many distractions, and too many disruptions can squander your energy and ruin your best intentions.

So be honest. If your lack of action is at least partially caused by your lack of organization, it's time to get your act together. If you need help with this, you might want to contact the National Association of Professional Organizers (you can visit their website at www.napo.net).

Stay Open to Life's Possibilities

Taking action to overcome fear isn't a one-shot deal. Each day there's always the possibility of setting off on new activities. Refuse to let fear rule your behavior. If you wait until all your uncertainties have resolved, you'll wait forever. Staying open to life's possibilities means that you can take action regardless of the fear you feel. As St. Francis of Assisi said, "Start by doing what's necessary, then what's possible, and suddenly you are doing the impossible."

PART THREE

Life after Fear

13

Fear Less, Live More: True Stories of Metamorphosis

The great thing in this world is not so much where we are, but in what direction we are moving.

—Oliver Wendell Holmes

Listen to how Marilyn describes her odyssey from Then to Now—a dozen ways in which her life has improved after using my program to overcome fear.

Back then I was afraid to admit I was afraid. Now I know that feelings aren't right or wrong, they just *are*, and that's okay.

Back then I worried that everything needed to be perfect. Now I know that "good enough" is good enough.

Back then life was exhausting and I was a bundle of nerves, always worrying about what might go wrong. Now I know that life is full of surprises. I can't prevent the unexpected from happening, so why make that my mission?

Back then I got so wrapped up in pleasing other people that I never thought about what I wanted. Now I give at least equal consideration to what I what and I notice I feel a lot less resentful.

Back then all the horrors I imagined were worse than any reality I experienced. Now I don't expect a catastrophe to plop down on my doorstep anytime soon, but if it did, I trust that somehow I'd be able to deal with it.

Back then I was addicted to watching TV tragedies and scare stories. Now I know that those programs are hazardous to my health and I watch them only in very limited doses.

Back then I made the mistake of thinking my husband would be my superhero, and he'd rescue me from disaster. (Boy, was I disappointed!) Now I know that I don't need a superhero, and I don't need to be rescued. Yet it's heartening to know that my husband and I watch out for each other.

Back then my idea of a wild time was soaking in a Jacuzzi. Now I'm looking forward to a cross-country trip.

Back then I would worry all the time about my son's safety as he flew around the world. Now I know that as much as I would like to protect him, I can't. I let him live his life and he's happier now that I've started to live mine.

Back then I always played it safe. Now I'm not afraid to go out on a limb. The fruit there can be really quite delicious!

Back then I felt I had few choices in life. Now I believe that the opportunities that are available to me are nothing short of spectacular.

Back then I was afraid of dying. Now I'm too busy living to worry about the day my life will end.

How Will Life Be Different When You Master Your Fears?

Marilyn's description of how her life has improved is a moving testament to the satisfactions and delights she discovered once fear no longer dominated her life. I've heard similar accounts from many others—people who have taken steps they once considered impossible; people who have moved beyond their greatest fears; people who are pleased, even astonished, by the new richness they find in their day-to-day life.

By implementing the skills you've learned in this book, you, like Marilyn, can make significant changes to your attitudes and behaviors. You can even reach a point where you feel that your whole character structure has changed. You can arrive at a place in which your response to fear is completely different from what it was before.

Do these changes mean that you feel no fear? No! I'd never wish that on you. Fear is a necessary emotion that's vital to your safety. What I do wish for you, however, is that you don't continue to live your life in fear. That you become more willing to take risks. That your life becomes richer, juicier, fuller, and more carefree. That you smile more and worry less. And—on those rare occasions when fear *does* visit you—that it's less intense and that, like all good visitors, it knows when it's time to take its leave.

Moreover, I hope that over time you learn to welcome change rather than let it terrify you. That you imagine good endings to upcoming events rather than automatically believe they will end badly. That you can connect with people who are less fearful than you and use them as role models. That you dare to imagine how their easygoing nature, their confidence, and their calm might rub off on you.

In short, I hope that taming your fears can result in a major shift for you: a new way to live in the world, a significant transformation. Here are some of the changes I consider likely:

- You'll make decisions that are no longer based on fear.

- You'll feel more empowered to cope with almost anything in life.

- You'll have more energy to do what you want to do.

- You'll celebrate a new, more confident you.

- You'll develop more assured relationships with others.

- You'll open up to a greater variety of experiences.

- You'll delight in a more optimistic, joyful, adventurous way of living.

As you consolidate, rehearse, and reinforce what you've learned, you'll reach the point where you'll be proud of the growth you've attained. You'll be delighted with the changes you've made. You'll be excited about your future. You'll be eager to see how you can handle challenging situations. You'll be grateful for what you've learned. You'll be confident about yourself. And you'll be more likely to embrace risks precisely because the rewards can be so satisfying.

Life after Fear

It's tempting to divide people into two groups of the self-assured and the fearful, as though these labels indicate categorically how people are and always will be. In fact, the real picture is far different. We often start out in one state of mind but end up in another. I know that's been true for me, and I know it's true for others. We are capable of change. We can learn new ways of living and leave our fears behind.

What follows are the stories of people who made the transition from fear and self-doubt to courage and confidence. In their own words, they speak about what made the difference, what motivated them to change, and how overcoming a fearful lifestyle changed who they are.

Angie: The Way It Was, the Way It Is

As a kid, I was afraid of lots of things—especially my father, who was an angry, abusive man. These fears dominated my life, making me afraid to speak up for myself or make a decision on my own. I'd be scared to death if someone was angry with me, especially if it was a man. Perhaps I'd still be in that position if I didn't have a traumatic experience in my life that became a turning point for me.

I was walking to the parking lot after work when I began to think that something was wrong. When I turned around, there was a clearly demented guy behind me. I was terrified, totally gripped with fear. I froze, unable to say anything. I couldn't even yell for help. Lucky for me, all he did was grab my purse and run off. It happened so quickly. Later, when I reported the incident to the security personnel, I became furious because they implied that the incident may have been my fault.

I decided that I wouldn't allow myself to end up in that kind of helpless, vulnerable, position again. I did two things that made a big difference in my life. I started therapy with a caring, confident psychologist who became a role model for me. She helped me understand how my relationship with my father influenced how passive I am in situations where I should be more assertive. The second thing I did was to take a women's martial arts course. I'm not naïve enough to believe I can now fight off any attackers, but I do believe that the techniques and attitude I've learned have made me so much more confident and outspoken that I think fewer people would mess with me in the first place.

Will: A Unique Antidote to Fear

I know it sounds strange to say, but hang gliding has been my antidote to fear. I've always worried about many things—supporting my family, being successful, getting sick, or someone in my family getting sick. I used to shy away from anything that was challenging. Now, however, when I'm apprehensive, I picture myself in my kite. Crazy as that sounds, it changes my whole attitude. If I can jump off a mountain top and soar like a bird, I can do anything.

A lot of people ask me how I ever began hang gliding, since I'm not well known as a courageous guy. I think the answer to that is simple: it's something I've always wanted to do. I was petrified the first time I went up, but I decided that regardless of what I was feeling in my body, I would rely on my training, equipment, and intense concentration. I focused only on what I needed to do and refused to be distracted by other thoughts—like dying.

I also need to give credit to a great instructor who helped me calm down by joking around and making it all sound so easy. Experience, practice, training, and supportive peers all contributed to easing the fear I felt. I still get a big adrenaline kick when I fly—I think that's why I do it—but overall the best benefit to me is that it makes me feel more in control of my life.

Jennie: Enough Fear for Now, Thank You

It should have been a great vacation at a beautiful resort, but I arrived home shaken. I wanted so much to have a good time but my fears kept getting in the way. I decided I had to do something before my fears ruined my life.

My husband likes to do adventurous things, but I was always holding him back. The only thing I was comfortable doing on vacation was sitting by the pool. Finally, one morning, I consented to go snorkeling with him. It started off fine. But once I got in the water, I was afraid. I couldn't go away from the shore because I needed to have my feet touch the ground. So while everyone else was having fun exploring further out, I was alone and miserable. Their reassurances that I couldn't drown with a life vest on did nothing to calm me down. My heart was racing, my breathing was rapid, and I felt disoriented and completely unsure of what I was doing. I finally left the water feeling defeated.

When we returned home, I took an inventory of how fear has limited my life. During college, I passed up a semester abroad because I dreaded being so far away from home. Even as an adult, I've always needed to live close to my parents. I've also chosen jobs because they seemed safe and nonthreatening, even though I considered them boring. I decided I needed to face my fears. I didn't want to live life like this.

I found a swimming instructor I could trust. I took a series of lessons until I felt more confident in the water. Well, that took care of the summer season. Once the winter season began, I decided I didn't want to be the only one in my crowd who didn't ski. So I took some skiing lessons. Right now, I can't handle more than the bunny slope, but I have to admit I actually enjoy going down the slope, even though I know I'm still too careful.

These days, I've become absolutely adamant about not letting fear control my life. My husband is interviewing for a new job in a neighboring state. If he gets that, I want to be able to move. I also don't want to handicap my son with my fears. So I have a lot of motivation to change. One of the ways I'm different now is that I picture myself succeeding at an activity rather than constantly rehashing all the possible pitfalls. If I begin to feel the panic, I've learned to calm myself down with self-reflection, saying such things as "Jen, you know you can do it. Take a deep breath, relax. It's going to be okay."

Gabe: Impossible Expectations

I'm an acupuncturist. When I started my practice, I had no money, no patients, and no experience running a business. I'd be alone in my office and feel paralyzed by fear that seemed like a deep dread of the unknown. I was constantly on edge. I kept wondering when this fear would stop and when patients would start coming. I was baffled about why people weren't jumping at the opportunity to come to my practice. I was wired, overtired, and grim about the whole thing.

Since then I've realized that the worst thing about my fears is that they prevent me from doing things. Making a decision isn't easy for me. I'm a big-time procrastinator and feel disappointed a lot because I demand that everything should fall right into place even when I haven't done anything to make that happen. After taking a course on time management, I realized that I spend so much time organizing things that I don't actually do anything.

After awhile I became aware of the obvious—that people weren't coming to my office because I was doing nothing to market myself. I was just expecting it all to magically happen. I decided I had to come out of my self-imposed isolation. I took a course on how to develop your practice and began to network with doctors who might refer patients to me.

Now I know that taking risks is essential for me. I can't hide out in my office. When I'm wired, I know I need to calm myself down, so I take walks, I meditate, I communicate. I view challenges as an opportunity to learn and grow. When I'm going through a difficult time, I can say—and believe—that this too shall pass.

Maria: Viewing Cancer through a Wide-angle Lens

This year has been the most terrifying year of my life. I was diagnosed with breast cancer. Since then I've been through surgery, chemo, and radiation. I'm not going to say that what I've been through hasn't been traumatic—it has. But I've gotten through it and I never would have believed that I could. I dealt with everything better than I could have anticipated. And—the best news of all—my doctors say I'm doing well and have a good chance of no recurrence.

During this time I've had to learn how to keep my fears in check and stay focused on the positive. Not always easy, but it's amazing that when I start to feel afraid and alone, my phone rings or I get an e-mail or a card from one of my friends and that has a big effect on lifting my spirits. Some friends have sent me beautiful music, which has been wonderful. Others send books, flowers, food, or other gifts that help me appreciate how many people are cheering me on.

Being the control freak that I am, it's been quite an adjustment to not be able to control this disease or the treatment. I've had to let go of being in charge and put all my trust in my medical team and follow their directions. I'm a very active person and one of the hardest things about cancer is that your life gets really boring. Everything is pretty much waiting. Waiting for blood tests, waiting to feel better, waiting for my energy to return, waiting for my life back. Waiting is very hard for someone like me. But now the treatment is over and I'm getting back to a somewhat normal life.

At the worst times I've had to have faith that a better tomorrow will come. I'm hoping that this cancer crisis will eventually become an event in my life rather than entirely take over my life as it has done this last year. Thinking that way helps me quiet my fears and take in the good around me.

Progress, Not Perfection

Courage isn't the absence of fear, but rather the judgment that something is more important than fear.

—AMBROSE REDMOON

As these stories indicate, you don't have to be an extraordinary person to overcome your fears. You don't have to be heroic, much less superhuman. Many of the most remarkable achievements are a consequence of perseverance and day-to-day willpower, not some special quality or talent. The goal to seek is progress, not perfection.

When you start to change, you may not feel very different at the outset. You may even be discouraged and wonder if you're changing at all. Be assured that you are—and probably in ways that exceed what you can imagine.

At some point, looking back, you'll be able to perceive the distance you've traveled without having been fully aware of all the steps you've taken. You'll see changes you made that you didn't even think were possible. I hope that you'll take pride in your accomplishments and recognize and celebrate all that you've done.

Here are some final thoughts I'd like to leave you with as you continue on your journey toward a more active, energetic, animated life.

- Whatever you think your parents should have done for you during your childhood to help you get past your fears, do for yourself now.

- Whatever you think your parents should have told you to help build your confidence, tell yourself now.

- Fear grows in isolation, so don't forget to talk to someone about your fears—someone who will listen openly and with understanding.

- Fear also grows in darkness. Shed light on your fears by learning more about what's frightening you. Do not, however, carry this advice to the extreme. Light is good, but dazzling spotlights can blind you.

- Welcome opportunities to be courageous—like a muscle, courage grows stronger with consistent use.

- Don't judge yourself too harshly. Remember that there's always another chance to get it right.

- You don't have to prove yourself to anyone but yourself. The question to ask is, "Am I satisfied with my efforts?" If your answer is yes, that's all that matters.

- A better life doesn't take superhuman effort. A bit of self-discipline and a sprinkling of courage can take you a long, long way.

- To live in fear is to waste precious time. Use the time you have in a way you won't regret.

- Life involves numerous disappointments. Don't add to this problem by letting your fears stop you from doing the things you want to do.

- Invest in your personal growth. You'll know it has paid off when you can say with joy, "Yes, I can do that! Yes, I've achieved that! Yes—and I'm so proud of myself."

- Explore, dream, and discover. In the words of Maya Angelou, "Life loves to be taken by the lapel and told, 'I'm with you kid. Let's go!'"

14

Other Approaches
to Help You
Master Your Fears

IT'S POSSIBLE THAT YOU, LIKE MANY PEOPLE, have been successful in taming your fears by implementing the ideas and exercises I've described throughout this book. But what if you've read this book, you agree with its concepts, you've done the exercises, and yet—despite trying hard to make them work—you're still at an impasse? What if you're making minimal progress, you're going around in circles, or your fears are getting more intense? What might you do?

Here are some options.

Psychotherapy

Psychotherapy offers many people the possibility of enriching their lives in a way that is unique. It can help you reduce the intensity and frequency of your fears as well as expand your coping skills. It can assist you with learning to cope with specific fears or with a pervasive fearful lifestyle. It can help you minimize your stress, increase your self-confidence, and clarify your thinking. And that is only the beginning. Long-term therapy can turn your life around—from one that's plagued with worries and apprehension to one that's full of joyful possibilities. How does all this happen?

There's no simple answer to this question. There are many types of psychotherapy and varying therapeutic orientations. In this section, I'd like to differentiate between two different models of therapy.

The Educational Model

This approach is based on the principles of learning. If you learned to be excessively fearful you can also learn not to be. There are many types of therapies that fall into the educational model, including:

- Behavior-modification therapy zeros in on reducing fears by positive reinforcement and desensitization.
- Cognitive therapy centers on changing fearful thinking and irrational beliefs.
- Psychodynamic therapy emphasizes the influence of current relationships, childhood experiences, and intrapsychic conflict.
- Family therapy brings in other family members and focuses on familial relationships.

Each approach has its own theoretical beliefs and techniques, and no one school of therapy is best for everyone. Hence, many therapists are eclectic. This means they use strategies from different schools of psychotherapy to best meet their clients' needs. It also means, however, that you may need to put time and energy into finding a therapist whom you feel you can work with effectively. Don't hesitate to ask potential therapists about the type of therapy they practice and what their approach to your problem would be.

The Medical Model

This approach is based on a mental disease paradigm. A diagnosis is made based on specific diagnostic criteria, and treatment often includes psychotropic medications as well as psychotherapy. Here is a descriptive overview of the major diagnoses that relate to fear.

GENERALIZED ANXIETY DISORDER

People with this disorder feel excessive anxiety, worry about many things in their lives, and have little ability to control the anxiety.

Typical symptoms include feeling keyed up or on edge, difficulty concentrating, mind going blank, restless sleep or insomnia, feeling irritable, prone to fatigue, and tense.

PANIC DISORDER

People who are diagnosed with this disorder have recurrent unexpected panic attacks. A panic attack is a period of intense fear that develops abruptly and usually reaches a peak within ten minutes. Frequent symptoms include pounding or racing heart, sweating, trembling, shortness of breath, chest pains, nausea, feeling light-headed, unsteadiness, feeling of unreality, and fear of losing control, of dying, or of going crazy. People who have had a panic attack usually worry about having another one, thus creating a vulnerability for agoraphobia (fear of leaving one's house or comfort zone).

SOCIAL PHOBIA

Social phobia is a strong and consistent fear of social situations, particularly those situations that have a performance aspect to them. Excessive self-consciousness provokes worry about being judged, embarrassed, and humiliated. Social phobias are usually intensified in unfamiliar situations or with people one does not know well.

SPECIFIC PHOBIAS

Unreasonable and excessive fear can be generated not only by social situations but also by specific objects or environments. Common phobias are fear of flying, fear of blood, fear of injections, fear of a specific type of animal, fear of water, fear of driving, fear of height, fear of closed places, fear of the dark, and fear of being alone. Some of these fears are rooted in experience; others are not.

ACUTE STRESS DISORDER

If a person has experienced, witnessed, or was confronted with an event that involved death (or near-death), serious injury, or psychological trauma, it's normal and predictable to feel some anxiety. However, if the fearful response is intense and involves strong feelings of helplessness, horror, being in a daze or feeling numb, detached, or "out of it," a diagnosis of acute stress disorder is made.

Post-Traumatic Stress Disorder (PTSD)

If the symptoms of acute stress disorder continue for more than ten months, the diagnosis is changed to post-traumatic stress disorder. Symptoms of PTSD include recurrent and intrusive upsetting thoughts, images, or nightmares of the event. Other symptoms include excessive avoidance of anything associated with the event, difficulty concentrating, irritability, outbursts of anger or tears, difficulty sleeping, feeling easily startled, and hypervigilance.

Obsessive-Compulsive Disorder

Obsessions are disturbing and intrusive thoughts that one can't stop thinking about. Compulsions are repetitive behaviors that one feels driven to do in response to an obsession. Common compulsions are excessive checking, insistence on things being in order, hand washing, or repetitive counting. People with OCD must act out their compulsions in a rigid way that seems excessive or inappropriate to others.

Depression

Though the major symptoms of depression are feelings of hopelessness, helplessness, worthlessness, low energy, fatigue, poor appetite, or overeating, it isn't unusual for depressed people to feel anxious, worried, tense, and nervous. Emotions rarely fit neatly into one distinct category.

Psychotropic Medications

Just as there are many types of psychotherapy, there are many types of psychotropic medications that may help reduce your anxiety, calm your nerves, and make you feel less stressed out. These drugs act primarily on the central nervous system, where they affect such diverse mental functions as mood, attention, energy, and cognition.

The major categories of medicines for anxiety disorders are antianxiety medications (such as Xanax and Klonopin) and antidepressants (SSRIs such as Prozac and Paxil, as well as CNS stimulants such as Wellbutrin and Zyban).

Antianxiety medications are generally prescribed for the symptomatic management of acute anxiety disorders and panic disorder. They work quickly and do not stay in your system for a long period of time. They can be prescribed to be taken daily or on an as-needed basis. In contrast, antidepressants, which are also useful for the management of anxiety disorders, may take several weeks until they begin working. They need to be taken on a daily basis and, when discontinuing use, should be tapered off rather than abruptly discontinued.

When treating anxiety or depression, medications work best in conjunction with psychotherapy.

Alternative Fear Busters

In addition to psychotherapy and medication, I'd like to suggest other alternative approaches that many people find valuable in taming their fears.

Biofeedback

Biofeedback is the technique of utilizing sensitive monitoring devices to give you information about your autonomic bodily function (such as heart rate or muscular tension). The goal is to gain some voluntary control over that function in order to help you become less tense, less anxious, and less fearful. When biofeedback is used in conjunction with guided imagery, it gives you an opportunity to develop the skill that will let you relax both your nervous system and your muscular system.

Yoga and Other Eastern-Style Therapies

Although based on a five-thousand-year-old Indian tradition, yoga has "gone mainstream" in recent decades. A wide variety of methods now allow you to reap the benefits of yoga. Popular schools of yoga include Kripalu, Kundalini, Integral, Ashtanga, Iyengar, and many others. Such courses are now widely available in gyms, adult-ed classes, and private studios. All of these approaches emphasize relaxing the body, calming the mind, cultivating internal strengths, and facilitating the flow of energy.

In addition to yoga, other eastern disciplines (such as "hard" and "soft" martial arts, including t'ai chi, chi kung, feng shui, karate, and jujitsu) can be useful and helpful in bolstering your confidence and taming your fears.

Massage

Massage has become a widely available method for easing physical tensions, quieting your mind, and relaxing your body from tip to toe. Massage has the advantage of your not having to do anything active—no instructions, no skills to learn, no looking at your neighbor and wondering if you're measuring up. If you can imagine taking it easy, unwinding, and letting go of your burdens, while being pampered with oils, fragrance, music, and just the right touch, you'll know why I highly recommend massage as a way to ease your fears.

Resistance to Psychotherapy

Some people are resistant to psychotherapy because they think they must be strong at all times and be able to pull themselves up by their bootstraps. Or they may worry that seeking psychotherapy means that something's wrong with them—they must be sick or crazy. Thank goodness these attitudes are not as prevalent as they used to be! Most people now know that seeking treatment for your emotional difficulties isn't a sign of weakness; on the contrary, it's a sign that you're strong enough and wise enough and healthy enough to acknowledge that there is a problem and that you want to resolve it.

Here's an analogy. If you had a physical health problem, would you try to treat it on your own? Well—maybe. Let's say that you have a cough that's been bothering you. No big deal; just give it some time or take some cough medicine. But if it's been bothering you for a while, or it's excessive in strength or frequency, it makes good sense to seek help from a doctor, otherwise the problem could turn into something worse. If you don't have the knowledge, skills, or expertise to treat a difficulty on your own, it is smart to seek assistance from someone who can help you. The same holds true for psychological and emotional issues.

Now let's say it's not that you're resistant to psychotherapy but someone in your life isn't supporting you, saying, "I don't believe in therapy" or "Just snap out of it." Well, remember what I said earlier in the book: "Whose voice are you going to listen to?"

Resistance to Medications

Some people love nothing better than popping a pill to make things better. Others go to the opposite extreme, refusing to take medication even when it can be quite beneficial. They think of medication as a crutch and would rather suffer with the symptoms than "give in" to taking drugs. Still others will be adamantly opposed to prescription medication but will take natural herbs in the mistaken belief that herbs have no side effects or that supplements cannot be harmful. A few people are resistant to medication because they once tried it and it did not sit well with them. Today, there are a lot more medications on the market than ever before. And it might be that your original prescription was not the best one for you. The right medication with the right dosage can make all the difference.

Though I wouldn't suggest medication as your only approach to reducing your fears, I know it can be useful for many people. Indeed, if you are too nervous, too frightened, or too jittery, it will be difficult for you to gain much benefit from psychotherapy or to implement the skills I have presented in this book.

Resistance to Alternative Approaches

Fearful people are often excessively cautious. You may be resistant to trying new techniques, especially ones that you may consider on the fringe or from another culture. I urge you to keep an open mind to the approaches I have mentioned. They are all well-established methods of preventative and therapeutic health care, even if a few of them are relatively new to mainstream America.

Not every approach will be good for every person. But how do you know if it will be beneficial for you unless you're willing at least to learn more about it? There may be immense, hidden treasures where you least expect to find them.

Resources

Dr. Linda Sapadin
Phone: (516) 791-2780
Fax: (516) 791-2568
Web: www.DrSapadin.com
www.psychwisdom.com

Dr. Sapadin is a psychologist, author, columnist, distinguished lecturer, consultant, and workshop leader. She specializes in helping individuals and groups overcome self-defeating patterns of living. Her Web sites provide information about her speaking engagements, learning seminars, and private practice, as well as excerpts from her books and copies of her weekly columns.

American Academy of Child and Adolescent Psychiatry
3615 Wisconsin Avenue, N.W.
Washington, D.C. 20016-3007
Phone: (202) 966-7300
Fax: (202) 966-2891
www.aacap.org

The American Academy of Child and Adolescent Psychiatry is an organization of psychiatrists who assist parents and families in understanding developmental, behavioral, emotional, and mental disorders affecting children and adolescents.

American Psychiatric Association
1000 Wilson Boulevard, Suite 1825
Arlington, VA 22209
Phone: (888) 35-PSYCH or (703) 907-7300
www.psych.org

The American Psychiatric Association is a national organization of psychiatrists whose members seek to ensure humane psychiatric treatment and appropriate, effective medication for persons with mental disorders.

American Psychological Association
750 First Street, N.E.
Washington, D.C. 20002-4242
Phone: (800) 374-2721 or (202) 336-5510
TDD/TTY: (202) 336-6123
www.apa.org
www.helping.apa.org/therapy

The American Psychological Association (APA) is a national organization of psychologists with a mission to educate, advocate, and promote psychotherapy and research that will expand the understanding of human emotions and behavior. They have developed an award-winning national education campaign ("Talk to Someone Who Can Help") that informs the public on when and how to seek help for specific emotional difficulties. Their goal is to ensure that those struggling to cope in these increasingly stressful times have the knowledge to make an informed decision regarding psychological treatment and care.

Anxiety Disorders Association of America
8730 Georgia Avenue, Suite 600
Silver Spring, MD 20910
Phone: (240) 485-1001
Fax: (240) 485-1035
www.adaa.org

The Anxiety Disorders Association of America (ADAA) is an educational organization that provides resources for anxiety disorder sufferers, family members, and the general public. They provide referrals to therapists and have a catalog of available brochures, books, and audiovisuals on anxiety disorders and related issues.

Freedom From Fear
308 Seaview Avenue
Staten Island, NY 10305
Phone: (718) 351-1717
www.freedomfromfear.com

Freedom from Fear is a national not-for-profit mental health advocacy organization whose mission is to provide information and referrals to individuals and their families who suffer from anxiety and depressive illnesses.

National Institute of Mental Health
NIMH Public Inquiries
6001 Executive Boulevard, Room 8184, MSC 9663
Bethesda, MD 20892-9663
Phone: (301) 443-4513
Fax: (301) 443-4279
TTY: (301) 443-8431
www.nimh.nih.gov

The National Institute of Mental Health is a governmental organization that sponsors research to help promote further understanding of mental illness. They are also a good source of information about the symptoms, diagnosis, and treatment of all types of mental illness.

National Mental Health Association
2001 N. Beauregard Street, 12th Floor
Alexandria, VA 22311
Phone: (703) 684-7722
Mental Health Resource Center: (800) 969-NMHA
TTY: (800) 433-5959
Fax: (703) 684-5968
www.nmha.org

National Mental Health Association is the country's oldest and largest not-for-profit organization addressing all aspects of mental health and mental illness through advocacy, education, research, and service.

NYS Society for Clinical Social Work
Empire State Building
350 Fifth Avenue, Suite 3308
New York, NY 10118
Phone: (800) 288-4279
E-mail: Sheila2688@aol.com
www.clinicalsw.org

In addition to providing educational programs and other informational services, this organization offers a psychotherapy referral service to clients through their web site.

NYU Social Work Action Network
www.nyu.edu/socialwork/wwwrsw/

The NYU Social Work Action Network has an abundance of materials for the public available through the organization's web site. Site visitors are immediately confronted with a key word search dialogue box that provides information on "fear," "anxiety," and "stress."

Obsessive-Compulsive Foundation
P.O. Box 9573
New Haven, CT 06535
Phone: (203) 315-2190
Fax: (203) 315-2196
E-mail: info@ocfoundation.org
www.ocfoundation.org/

The Obsessive Compulsive Foundation (OCF) is an international not-for-profit organization composed of people with obsessive-compulsive disorder (OCD) and others concerned about the illness. Their mission is to educate the public and professional communities about OCD, to provide assistance to those with OCD, and to support research regarding causes and treatment of OCD.

Further Reading

Antony, Martin M., and Richard P. Swinson. *The Shyness & Social Anxiety Workbook: Proven Techniques for Overcoming Your Fears.* Oakland, Calif.: New Harbinger, 2000.

Baer, L. *Getting Control: Overcoming Your Obsessions and Compulsions.* Boston: Little, Brown and Co., 1991.

Bemis, Judith, and Amy Barrada. *Embracing the Fear: Learning to Manage Anxiety & Panic Attacks.* Center City, Minn.: Hazelden, 1994.

Berent, Jonathan, and Amy Lemley. *Beyond Shyness: How to Conquer Social Anxieties.* New York: Fireside 1994.

Blakeslee, Mermer. *In the Yikes! Zone.* New York: Dutton, 2002.

Bourne, E. J. *The Anxiety and Phobia Workbook,* 2nd ed. Oakland, Calif.: New Harbinger Publications, 1995.

Carducci, Bernardo J. *Shyness: A Bold New Approach.* New York: HarperCollins, 1999.

Damasio, Antonio. *The Feeling of What Happens: Body and Emotion in the Making of Consciousness.* New York: Harvest Books, 2000.

———. *Looking for Spinoza: Joy, Sorrow, and the Feeling Brain.* New York: Harcourt, 2003.

Davis, Martha, et al. *The Relaxation and Stress Reduction Workbook.* Oakland, Calif.: New Harbinger, 2000.

Dayhoff, Signe A. *Diagonally-Parked in a Parallel Universe: Working Through Social Anxiety.* Placitas, N.M.: Effectiveness Plus Publishers, 2000.

DuPont, R. L., et al. *The Anxiety Cure.* New York: John Wiley and Sons, 1998.

Foa, E. B., and Wilson R. *Stop Obsessing! How to Overcome Your Obsessions and Compulsions.* New York: Bantam Books, 1991.

Freeman, Lynne. *Panic Free: Eliminate Anxiety/Panic Attacks without Drugs and Take Control of Your Life.* Denver, Colo.: Arden Books, 1999.

Glassner, Barry. *The Culture of Fear: Why Americans are Afraid of the Wrong Things*. New York: Basic Books, 2000.

Hallowell, E. M. *Worry*. New York: Ballantine Publishing Group, 1997.

Handly, Robert. *Anxiety and Panic Attacks: Their Cause and Cure: The Five-Point Life-Plus Program for Conquering Fear*, New York: Fawcett Crest, 1985.

Hart, Archibald. *The Anxiety Cure*. Nashville, Tenn.: Word Publishing, 2001.

Jeffers, Susan. *Feel the Fear and Do It Anyway*. New York: Fawcett Columbine, 1987.

LeDoux, Joseph. *The Emotional Brain: The Mysterious Underpinnings of Emotional Life*. New York: Touchstone Books, 1998.

———. *Synaptic Self: How Our Brains Become Who We Are*. New York: Viking Press, 2002.

Markway, Barbara G., Ph.D., and Gregory Markway, Ph.D. *Painfully Shy: How to Overcome Social Anxiety and Reclaim Your Life*. New York: St. Martin's Press, 2001.

Peurifoy, Reneau Z. *Anxiety, Phobias, and Panic: A Step-By-Step Program for Regaining Control of Your Life*. New York: Warner, 1995.

Rutledge, Thom. *Embracing Fear and Finding the Courage to Live Your Life*. San Francisco: HarperCollins, 2002.

Sapadin, Linda, with Jack Maguire. *Beat Procrastination and Make the Grade: The Six Styles of Procrastination and How Students Can Overcome Them*. New York: Penguin USA, 1999.

———. *It's about Time! The Six Styles of Procrastination and How to Overcome Them*. New York: Penguin USA, 1997.

Seligman, Martin E. *Authentic Happiness: Using the New Positive Psychology to Realize Your Potential for Lasting Fulfillment*. New York: Free Press, 2002.

———. *Learned Optimism: How to Change Your Mind and Your Life*. New York: Pocket Books, 1998.

Weekes, Claire. *Hope and Help for Your Nerves*. New York: Signet, 1991.

———. *Peace from Nervous Suffering*. New York: Signet, 1990.

Wilson, R. Reid, Ph.D. *Don't Panic: Taking Control of Anxiety Attacks*. New York: HarperCollins, 1996.

Index

actions, 171–189. *See also* change
  program; one gutsy thing principle; self-muscle exercise
  faking it, 186–189
  importance of, 171–172
  self-muscle exercise, 172–177
  virtual reality, 178–186
activities, restriction of, fearful
  lifestyle, 8
acute stress disorder, 225
adaptive response, fearful lifestyle
  as, quiz for, 13–14
adventures, 217–219
Alda, Alan, 169
amygdala, fear physiology, 138, 139
Angelou, Maya, 222
antianxiety medications, 226–227
antidepressant medications,
  226–227
anxiety reactions, 11
architectural design, 179
attitudes, 77–93. *See also* change
  program
  change process, 45–46
  difficulty, 80–86
  media exposure, 77–79
  out-of-body experience, 91–93
  resilience development, 86–89
  risk analysis, 79–80
  sense perceptions, 90–91

balance, body factors, 146–147
Baum, L. Frank, 196
biofeedback, 227
body factors, 135–154. *See also*
  change program
  balance, 146–147
  circuit breaker analogy, 153–154
  fear physiology, 138–141
  listening to, 147–149
  meditation, 147–151
  memory, 135–138
  overload reduction, 151–153

response styles, recognition of,
  141–145
body movements, incompatible
  thoughts and, 163–165
brain, fear physiology, 138–141
brainstorming, thinking skills, 64–66
breathing exercises, relaxation,
  155–157

cancer, 219–220
Carlyle, Thomas, 166
Center for Women and
  Achievement, 191
change process, 27, 43–50. *See also*
  change program; fearful
  lifestyle
  attitude in, 45–46
  concepts in, 44–45
  difficulties in, 47–49
  readiness, 49–50
change program, 51–210. *See also*
  actions; attitudes; body factors;
  change process; fearful lifestyle;
  language enhancement; one
  gutsy thing principle; relaxation; speech patterns; thinking
  skills
  actions, 171–189
  alternatives, 223–229
  attitudes, 77–93
  biofeedback, 227
  body factors, 135–154
  language enhancement, 95–114
  massage, 228
  medications, 226–227, 229
  one gutsy thing principle, 191–210
  progress in, 220–222
  psychotherapy, 22, 223–226
  relaxation, 155–169
  speech patterns, 115–133
  successful outcome examples,
    213–220
  thinking skills, 53–75

chi kung, 227
childhood. *See* developmental
    factors
children's books, 196–198
child's play, relaxation, 165–166
Chinese medicine, body factors, 148
choices, limiting of, fearful lifestyle,
    8
circuit breaker analogy, body
    factors, 153–154
Collier, Robert, 96
communication. *See* language
    enhancement
compliant fear style, described,
    24–25
computer simulation. *See* virtual
    reality
control, incremental fear reduction,
    160–161
controlling fear style
    described, 26–27
    paralysis of analysis, 60–61
Cooley, Mason, 60
cortisol, fear physiology, 139
criticism
    self-talk, language enhancement,
        106–111
    speech patterns, 129–132
current relationships, developmen-
    tal factors, 41–42

death of parent, developmental
    factors, 29, 30–31, 35
decision making, thinking skills,
    54–56
depression, 226
developmental factors, 29–42. *See
    also* fearful lifestyle
    family dynamics, 39
    parental expectations, 37–39
    parental responses to outside
        world, 39–40
    parental style, 33–37
    quiz for identification of, 37
    relationships, current, 41–42
    temperament and genetics, 32–33
    trauma, 30–32

Dewey, John, 173
difficulty, attitudes, 80–86
dramatic acting, self-muscle
    exercise, 173–174
driver-training, 178–179

Eastern cultures
    alternative therapies, 227
    body factors, 147–151
educational model, psychotherapy,
    224
Emerson, Ralph Waldo, 195
epinephrine, fear physiology, 139
excitement, constriction of, fearful
    lifestyle, 8
exercises. *See also* quizzes; relaxation
    balance, body factors, 146–147
    body movements and incompati-
        ble thoughts, 163–165
    body response styles, recognition
        of, 143–145
    breathing exercises, 155–157
    children's books, 198
    criticism, 132
    guided imagery, 184–186
    intuition, 169
    labeling of emotion, 121–122
    language enhancement strategies,
        111–114
    negative/positive voices, 118, 120
    obsessive thinking, 60
    one gutsy thing principle,
        203–207
    outcomes, 72–73
    paralysis of analysis thinking,
        62–64
    relaxation, 75
    sense perceptions, 90
    sentence endings, 129
    trigger words, 97–101
    voice development, 103–105
    what-if issues, 125–126
experience
    fearful lifestyle, 11–13
    learning through, 182–183
    one gutsy thing principle,
        199–202

exposure experience, learning through, 182–183

faking it, actions, 186–189
family dynamics, developmental factors, 39
fear, physiology of, 138–141
fearful lifestyle. *See also* change process; change program; developmental factors
  as adaptive response, quiz for, 13–14
  change program, 27
  compliant fear style, 24–25
  controlling fear style, 26–27
  damaging consequences of, 7–11
  definitions, 11–13
  development of, 29–42
  expression of, 11, 15–16
  gender differences, 15–16
  hypervigilant fear style, 23–24
  identification quizzes, 16–22
  macho fear style, 25–26
  shyness fear style, 22–23
fear of flying, attitudes, 92–93
feng shui, 227
Francis of Assisi, Saint, 210
frozen response style, body factors, 143
fun, constriction of, fearful lifestyle, 8

Gandhi, Mahatma, 132
gender differences, fearful lifestyle, 15–16
generalized anxiety disorder, 224–225
genetics, developmental factors, 32–33
Gide, André, 43
Goodrich, Ronald, 173
guided imagery, 183–186

hang gliding, 217–218
hardiness development, attitudes, 86–89
Harris, Corra, 49

hippocampus, fear physiology, 139
Holmes, Oliver Wendell, 213
Holocaust survivors
  developmental factors, 29
  resilience development, 86–87
homeostasis, body factors, 146–147
Horace (Roman poet), 93
hormones, fear physiology, 139
hypersensitive response style, body factors, 141–142
hypervigilant fear style
  described, 23–24
  obsessive thinking, 56
  relaxation, 73–74

ignorance, change process, 48–49
impulsiveness, intuition contrasted, 168
incremental fear reduction, 159–161
intuition
  change process, 49
  relaxation, 167–169

James, William, 77, 135, 187
Johnson, Samuel, 50
joy, constriction of, fearful lifestyle, 8
jujitsu, 227

karate, 227
Kennedy, John F., 39
Klonopin, 226

labeling of emotion, speech patterns, 120–123
Lagemann, John Kord, 167
language enhancement, 95–114. *See also* change program; speech patterns
  importance of, 95
  self-talk, 106–111
  state of mind, 96–101
  strategies for, 111–114
  voice development, 101–106
learning process
  change process, 48
  psychotherapy, 224

letter writing, 179–181
life experience. *See* experience
loss. *See* trauma

macho fear style
  described, 25–26
  outcomes, 70
MacLaine, Shirley, 113
maladaptive response, fearful
    lifestyle as, quiz for, 13–14
Marley, Bob, 167
martial arts, 217
massage, 228
media exposure
  attitudes, 77–79
  fear development, 140–141
  overload reduction, body factors,
    151–153
medical model, psychotherapy,
    224–226
medications
  resistance to, 229
  types of, 226–227
meditation, body factors, 147–151
memory, body factors, 135–138
Menninger, Karl, 48
mind management. *See* thinking
    skills
Moore, Mary Tyler, 202
muscle relaxation exercises,
    157–159
music, relaxation, 166–167

negative/positive voices, speech
    patterns, 117–120
Nehru, Jawaharlal, 77
new skill acquisition
  actions, 178, 217–219
  self-muscle exercise, 175–176
norepinephrine, fear physiology,
    139

obsession, thinking skills
    contrasted, 56–60
obsessive-compulsive disorder, 226
one gutsy thing principle, 191–210.
    See also actions; change program

children's books, 196–198
  concept of, 191–193
  examples of, 193–194
  readiness for, 195–196
  suggestions for, 199–210
organization, one gutsy thing
    principle, 209–210
outcomes, thinking skills, 69–73
out-of-body experience, attitudes,
    91–93
overload reduction, body factors,
    151–153
overprotective parental style, devel-
    opmental factors, 33–35
overreactive response style, body
    factors, 142–143

panic disorder, 225
panic reactions, 11
Pantanjali, 149
paradox, one gutsy thing principle,
    207–208
paralysis of analysis, avoidance of,
    thinking skills, 60–64
parenting
  developmental factors, 31–32
  family dynamics, developmental
    factors, 39
  parental expectations, develop-
    mental factors, 37–39
  parental style, developmental
    factors, 33–37
  responses to outside world,
    developmental factors, 39–40
Pascal, Blaise, 161
passivity, voice development, 106
pattern of experience. *See* experience
Paxil, 226
Peck, Sheila, 191
phobias, 11, 225
playfulness, relaxation, 165–166
positive/negative voices, speech
    patterns, 117–120
post-traumatic stress disorder
    (PTSD), 11, 226
prefrontal cortex, fear physiology,
    139

problem restatement, speech patterns, 123–126
progressive muscle relaxation exercises, 158–159
Prozac, 226
psychotherapy, 223–226
  educational model, 224
  medical model, 224–226
  resistance to, 228
psychotropic medications, 226–227

qigong, 151
quizzes. *See also* exercises
  fearful lifestyle as adaptive/ maladaptive response, 13–14
  fearful lifestyle identification, 16–22
  identification of developmental factors, 37

readiness
  change process, 49–50
  incremental fear reduction, 161
  one gutsy thing principle, 195–196
Redmoon, Ambrose, 220
reframing, thinking skills, 66–69
relationships, current, developmental factors, 41–42
relaxation, 155–169. *See also* change program
  body factors, 148–149
  body movements and incompatible thoughts, 163–165
  breathing exercises, 155–157
  incremental fear reduction, 159–161
  intuition, 167–169
  muscle exercises, 157–159
  music, 166–167
  playfulness, 165–166
  stillness, 161–163
  thinking skills, 73–75
resilience development, attitudes, 86–89
resistance
  incremental fear reduction, 161

medications, 229
psychotherapy, 228
stillness, 162
response styles, recognition of, body factors, 141–145
risk
  fearful lifestyle, 12–13
  parental style, developmental factors, 33–37
risk analysis, attitudes, 79–80
role models, parental style, developmental factors, 34, 35
role playing, 181–182
Roosevelt, Eleanor, 171, 191
Roosevelt, Franklin D., 7, 53
Roosevelt, Theodore, 86
Russell, Bertrand, 45
Russell, Harriet, 155

Schacter, Stanley, 36
self-muscle exercise, 172–177
  concept of, 173
  dramatic acting, 173–174
  fear identification, 177
  new skill acquisition, 175–176
  preparation for, 176–177
self-talk, language enhancement, 106–111
sense perceptions, attitudes, 90–91
sensory cortex, fear physiology, 139
sentence endings, speech patterns, 126–129
September 11 terrorism attack
  media exposure, 78
  parental responses to, developmental factors, 39–40
shyness fear style
  described, 22–23
  outcomes, 69–70
silence, speech patterns, 132–133
simplicity, one gutsy thing principle, 208–209
skill acquisition. *See* new skill acquisition
social phobia, 225
somatic factors. *See* body factors
Sophocles, 172

speech patterns, 115–133. *See also*
    change program; language
    enhancement
    criticism, 129–132
    fear descriptions, 115–117
    labeling of emotion, 120–123
    negative/positive voices,
        117–120
    problem restatement, 123–126
    sentence endings, 126–129
    silence, 132–133
state of mind, language enhance-
    ment, 96–101
stillness, relaxation, 161–163
stress disorder, acute, 225
stress hormones, fear physiology,
    139
subliminal knowledge, change
    process, 49

tae kwan do, 151
t'ai chi, 151, 227
temperament, developmental fac-
    tors, 32–33
tensing, muscle relaxation exer-
    cises, 157–159
terrorism
    media exposure, 78
    parental responses to, develop-
        mental factors, 39–40
thalamus, fear physiology, 139
thinking
    body movements and incompati-
        ble thoughts, 163–165
    fearful lifestyle, 7–8
    incremental fear reduction,
        159–161
thinking skills, 53–75. *See also*
    change program
    brainstorming, 64–66
    decision making, 54–56
    importance of, 53–54
    incremental fear reduction,
        159–161

obsession contrasted, 56–60
    outcomes, 69–73
    paralysis of analysis avoidance,
        60–64
    reframing, 66–69
    relaxation, 73–75
Toynbee, Arnold, 165
trauma
    developmental factors, 30–32
    parental responses to outside
        world, developmental factors,
        39–40
trigger words, language enhance-
    ment, 97–101
trust, parental style, developmental
    factors, 35
Twain, Mark, 110

underprotective parental style,
    developmental factors, 35–36

virtual reality, actions, 178–186
voice development, language
    enhancement, 101–106
Vos Savant, Marilyn, 91

Weeks, Edward, 27
Wellbutrin, 226
what-if issues, problem restate-
    ment, 124–126
Wilde, Oscar, 199
Wilson, Earl, 186
words. *See* language enhancement

Xanax, 226

yoga
    alternative therapies, 227
    body factors, 148

Zimbardo, Philip, 78
Zyban, 226